W9-BRY-662

VISUAL QUICKSTART GUIDE

JAVASCRIPT

FOR THE WORLD WIDE WEB

Ted Gesing
Jeremy Schneider

 Peachpit Press

Visual QuickStart Guide
JavaScript for the World Wide Web
Ted Gesing and Jeremy Schneider

Peachpit Press
2414 Sixth Street
Berkeley, CA 94710
510-548-4393
800-283-9444
510-548-5991 (fax)

Find us on the World Wide Web at:
http://www.peachpit.com

Peachpit Press is a division of Addison Wesley Longman

Copyright © 1997 by Ted Gesing and Jeremy Schneider

Editor: Kaethin Prizer
Cover design: The Visual Group
Inhouse production: Kate Reber

Notice of Rights
All rights reserved. No part of this book may be reproduced
or transmitted in any form by any means, electronic,
mechanical, photocopying, recording, or otherwise, without
the prior written permission of the publisher. For information on getting permission for reprints and excerpts, contact
Trish Booth at Peachpit Press.

Notice of Liability
The information in this book is distributed on an "As Is"
basis, without warranty. While every precaution has been
taken in the preparation of the book, neither the author nor
Peachpit Press, shall have any liability to any person or entity
with respect to any loss or damage caused or alleged to be
caused directly or indirectly by the instructions contained in
this book or by the computer software and hardware prod-
ucts described in it.

ISBN 0-201-68814-X

9 8 7 6 5 4 3 2 1

Printed and bound in the United States of America

Thank You.

John Kane, Charles Wachter, Stephanie Brenowitz,
Karen Jacobson, and our families.

Ted Nace, Kaethin Prizer, Kate Reber,
and the rest of the staff at Peachpit Press.

CONTENTS

INTRODUCTION

Nearly every magazine and newspaper in the world has reported on the potential of the World Wide Web. Supposedly, its inter activity will change the nature of communications. Only now, however, is this hype becoming reality. JavaScript, a powerful and easy-to-learn tool, brings true interactivity to the Web.

In the early '90s researchers developed the World Wide Web as a means of sharing information for scientific research. Its distinguishing feature, the hypertext link, allowed users to jump between documents.

As the Web has exploded into a commercial event, the demand for more publishing flexibility has followed suit. Browsers have moved beyond the static page into the realm of live video feeds and portable document formats.

But interactivity remains the essential promise of the Web. Beyond the hypertext link, JavaScript allows for the creation of web pages which truly respond to user actions. The Web is not about broadcasting; it is about shaping the experience of the individual user. JavaScript makes this happen.

JavaScript and Java

The public has largely confused JavaScript and Java, but their uses and levels of difficulty are actually quite different.

The most basic difference between Java and JavaScript is that Java is a full-scale programming language and JavaScript is an easy-to-use scripting language. With Java, you can create applets which are embedded within a web page or even stand-alone applications. By integrating JavaScript into your HTML, you can make the elements of a web page respond to user actions.

The two languages do share a common root, however, as their names suggest. The same company, Sun Microsystems, endorses the two languages, and they share syntax and structure. Additionally, JavaScript is able to control and share information with Java applets.

Typical Java uses:

1. Creating a game which runs in a browser window.

2. Creating interactive web graphics. See Figure 1.

3. Writing stand-alone applications.

Typical JavaScript uses:

1. Customizing a page based on the user's browser version.

2. Providing visual feedback to user actions. See Figure 2.

3. Checking for mistakes in forms before they are submitted.

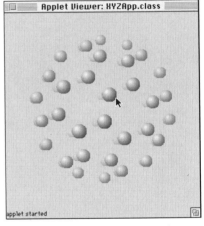

Figure 1 Here a Java applet allows the user to control a three-dimensional model with the mouse.

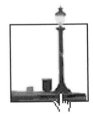

Figure 2 Here JavaScript changes an image when the user moves the cursor over it.

Script 1 JavaScript is integrated with HTML code. Throughout the scripts in this book, an arrow(→) indicates that we have wrapped what should be a single line in your script.

```
                    script
<HTML>
<HEAD>
<TITLE>Say hi with JavaScript</TITLE>
<SCRIPT LANGUAGE="JavaScript">
<!--HIDE
function sayHi(field) {
    var name = field.value
    alert("Hi, " + name + "!")
}
//STOP HIDING-->
</SCRIPT>
</HEAD>
<BODY>
<FORM>
<INPUT TYPE="text" VALUE="Enter name here"
→onChange="sayHi(this)">
</FORM>
</BODY>
</HTML>
```

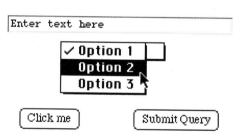

Figure 3 JavaScript can interact with the user through these common form elements.

A SCRIPTING LANGUAGE

The term *scripting language* has no strict definition. Scripting languages combine tools from programming languages to make them more concise and usable. Having fewer features makes them less versatile, but they are easy enough for non-programmers to learn and master.

JavaScript is a scripting language designed to extend the functionality of web pages. Typically written as part of an HTML document, a script controls the elements of the page and reacts to user actions.

JavaScript uses simple commands which manipulate the parts of a web page, such as the form elements in Figure 3. Throughout this book you will find practical examples which illustrate these building blocks. Once you become comfortable with the basics, you can combine them to create the scripts you want for your site.

You can base your scripts on the samples next to the text. Within the sample scripts, an arrow (→) indicates that we have wrapped what you should type as a single line.

In addition, we highlight in red the lines of script which illustrate each page's particular topic. We examine these lines in greater detail in the adjoining text column. Here, we reprint each line in red, then we isolate the line's individual components (now in black type) with a short paragraph explaining the purpose of each element.

CLIENT-SIDE PROCESSING

The most common way to extend the abilities of a web page is through the Common Gateway Interface (CGI). CGI programs run on a web server and deliver information to the user as a new page.

In many ways, JavaScript is a client-side replacement for CGI. This means that you can now process information on the user's computer instead of a web server. While certain pages, such as search engines, still need to access the server, many can run independently on the client machine.

Sending information across the lines and servers of the Internet slows down its use. Client-side processing helps to reduce these bottlenecks.

The advantages of client-side processing:

1. **More Speed.** Because there is no need to cross the slow lines of the Internet, your only limitation is the speed of the client machine.

2. **Less burden on the web server.** CGI applications can drain a server's processing power and even lead to crashes. Client-side processing uses no more of the server's resources than downloading a normal page.

3. **Less network traffic.** Widespread use of client-side processing increases the speed of the Internet as a whole. The more people use it, the less time you'll spend waiting for pages to download.

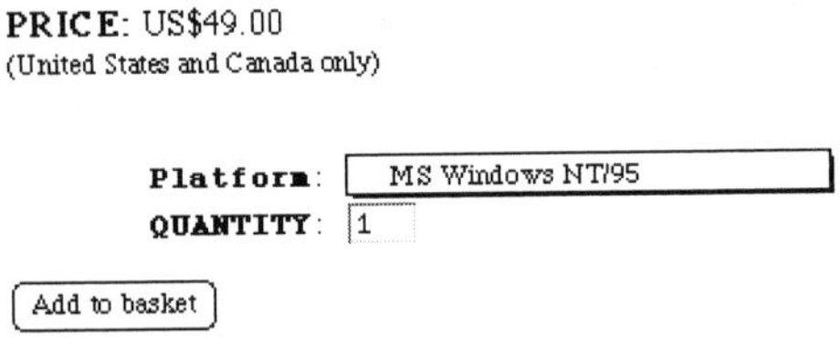

PRICE: US$49.00
(United States and Canada only)

Platform: MS Windows NT/95
QUANTITY: 1

Add to basket

Figure 4 CGI scripts are commonly used to search databases, store user registration information, and accept credit card information.

Figure 5 CGI depends on the server to process information.

Figure 6 JavaScript uses the client computer to process information.

CLIENT-SIDE PROCESSING

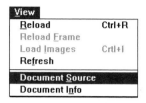

Figure 7 Scripts are usually contained within the HTML document and can be viewed easily.

VIEWING A JAVASCRIPT SCRIPT

The instructions you write in JavaScript are known as *code*. Before a computer can read code it has to be *compiled* or converted to instructions that the computer understands.

With most programming languages, the person or software company that writes the code compiles it to work with a specific platform (Windows, Macintosh, etc.). Like HTML, however, JavaScript is downloaded as text. The user's computer compiles it as it downloads. This means that JavaScript is *platform-independent*. The scripts you write can run on Windows, Macintosh, or Unix machines.

Because scripts are downloaded as text, you can generally read them by viewing the HTML source. In addition to trying the scripts in this book, you should look at some real web sites and try their techniques.

To view a JavaScript script:

1. Select Document Source from the View menu in Netscape Navigator.

OR Select Source from the View menu in Internet Explorer.

2. Both browsers will open a second window containing the HTML document. Find the script which begins after the line <SCRIPT LANGUAGE="JavaScript">.

3. Examine the script to its end, marked by </SCRIPT>.

BROWSERS AND THEIR VERSIONS

Regardless of which browser you use, you should try to make your pages compatible with as many browsers as possible. The two market leaders both support JavaScript. You can find the differences in their implementations in Appendix C.

Netscape Navigator 3.0:

Before Sun entered the picture, Netscape developed JavaScript under the name Live-Script. Throughout the language's development Netscape has been on the cutting edge of JavaScript support.

Netscape Navigator™ 3.0

Navigator 2.0, the first JavaScript-compatible browser, has limited and buggy support for the scripting language. With 3.0, the company has vastly improved the reliability and power of JavaScript.

The vast majority of web users surf with Navigator. For this reason, we have emphasized its version of JavaScript. We have also included all of Navigator 3.0's new JavaScript features. See Appendix B for a complete listing.

Microsoft Internet Explorer 3.0:

Microsoft came fairly late to the browser game, but is quickly gaining market share.

Internet Explorer 3.0

In Explorer 3.0, Microsoft has introduced JavaScript support under the name JScript. Despite some differences, its implementation is basically the same as that in Navigator 2.0. You can assume that all Navigator 3.0 features do not work in Explorer and all Navigator 2.0 features do. Appendix C contains a listing of the exceptions to this rule.

JavaScript Basics

BBEdit Lite 3.5

emacs

Figure 1.1 You can use any text editor to write JavaScript scripts, but BBEdit (Macintosh) and Emacs (Unix and other platforms) are among the best.

WHERE TO WRITE YOUR SCRIPTS

Like HTML, JavaScript scripts are just text documents containing special words that your browser interprets. Because of this, you can write them in almost any text editor or word processor.

If you already use a text editor to write HTML, use the same one to write your scripts. Otherwise, you should consider BBEdit ($119) and BBEdit Lite (freeware) for the Macintosh, and the Programmers File Editor (freeware) for Windows. These editors have features and extensions that allow them to handle HTML and JavaScript better than a standard word processor.

To save time, you may want to write your scripts directly on the web server. In most cases this means using a UNIX text editor. Your best bet is Emacs, an extremely powerful application available on most UNIX machines.

INSERTING YOUR SCRIPT IN HTML

You will usually want to put your scripts directly in the HTML document of the desired page. To do this you use the script and end-script tags, which signal the beginning and end of a script.

You can place scripts in either the head or body portion of the page. As you become more experienced in JavaScript, you will want to put your scripts in the head so that they load first.

To insert your script in HTML:

1. <SCRIPT LANGUAGE="JavaScript">

<SCRIPT   >

Signal the beginning of your script with the script tag.

          LANGUAGE="JavaScript"

Specify that you are using the JavaScript language.

2. <!--HIDE

Type **<!--** to create an HTML comment. This prevents non-JavaScript browsers from trying to read your script, as in Figure 1.2.

3. Insert your script within the script and comment tags.

4. //STOP HIDING-->

Use an end-comment tag (**-->**) to allow other browsers to begin reading the document again. Put two slashes before it, to prevent JavaScript from reading this line (see page 13).

5. </SCRIPT>

Signal the end of your JavaScript code with the end-script tag.

Script 1.1 You use the script tags to include JavaScript code in an HTML document.

```
<HTML>
<HEAD>
<TITLE>Inserting JavaScript</TITLE>
</HEAD>
<BODY>
<H1>Does it work...
<SCRIPT LANGUAGE="JavaScript">
<!--HIDE
document.write("It works!")
//STOP HIDING-->
</SCRIPT>
</H1>
</BODY>
</HTML>
```

Figure 1.2 A JavaScript-capable browser reads the script, but others ignore it.

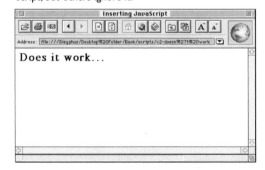

INSERTING YOUR SCRIPT IN HTML

Script 1.2 To use it in multiple pages, you can keep your script in a separate file.

```
<HTML>
<HEAD>
<TITLE>Inserting JavaScript</TITLE>
</HEAD>
<BODY>
<H1>The following script
<SCRIPT LANGUAGE="JavaScript"
→SRC="../other.js">
</SCRIPT>
```

```
    document.write(" is in a separate file.")
```

Table 1.1 Basic syntax for addressing file locations.

ADDRESS	WHAT IT MEANS
http://www.mysite.com/script.js	normal address
script.js OR ./script.js	same directory as HTML file
../script.js	one directory up from HTML file
.../script.js	two directories up from HTML file
/script.js	top level directory of domain

SCRIPTS IN SEPARATE FILES

Navigator 3.0 lets you keep your scripts in separate documents. You'll need to do this if you want to use the same script for several web pages or hide your code from users.

In order for the browser to read your script, you need to tell it where the file is located. You can do this with the source attribute in the script tag. When using separate source files you do not need to include the hide comments.

Before you can use external source documents, you should have your server administrator map the suffix .js to the MIME type **application/x-javascript**.

To put your script in a separate file:

1. <SCRIPT LANGUAGE="JavaScript" SRC="../other.js">

<SCRIPT LANGUAGE="JavaScript" >

Signal the beginning of your script with the script tag.

SRC=

Type **SRC=** to tell the browser that you are using a separate script document.

"../myScript.js"

Specify the location of your JavaScript document within quotation marks. You can use either a relative or absolute file location, as explained in Table 1.1. Your script file has to end with the suffix .js.

2. </SCRIPT>

Signal the end of your script with the end-script tag. You must include this even though you are not putting the script in the HTML document.

NON-JAVASCRIPT CONTENT

In addition to hiding your scripts from non-JavaScript browsers, you will probably want to display a message telling the user to get a better browser. You can do this with the noscript tag.

Navigator 3.0 ignores everything between the start and end-noscript tags. You can place any alternate content within these two tags.

Because the noscript tag is new to Navigator 3.0, it is not recognized by other browsers. As a result the text between the noscript tags will be displayed. The text is also displayed if JavaScript has been disabled by the user in the Network Preferences dialog box.

To include a message for non-JavaScript browsers:

1. <NOSCRIPT>

Insert the noscript tag before the alternate content.

2. <H2>This page requires a JavaScript-capable browser.</H2>

Type the desired message. Navigator 3.0 ignores everything within the noscript tags. Other browsers read it as standard HTML. Figure 1.3 illustrates this effect.

3. </NOSCRIPT>

Insert the end-noscript tag after your message. This tells Navigator 3.0 to continue reading the document.

Script 1.3 The noscript tag allows you to include alternate content for non-JavaScript browsers.

```
<HTML>
<HEAD>
<TITLE>NOSCRIPT example</TITLE>
</HEAD>
<BODY>
<SCRIPT LANGUAGE="JavaScript">
<!--HIDE
alert("Welcome to my JavaScript page!")
//STOP HIDING -->
</SCRIPT>
<NOSCRIPT>
<H2>This page requires a JavaScript-capable
browser.</H2>
</NOSCRIPT>
</BODY>
</HTML>
```

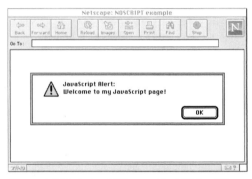

Figure 1.3 Navigator 3.0 ignores the HTML within the noscript tags, but other browsers display it.

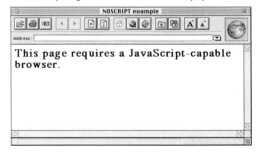

Script 1.4 Document.write() creates HTML code.

```
<HTML>
<HEAD>
<TITLE>Using document.write()</TITLE>
</HEAD>
<BODY>
<SCRIPT LANGUAGE="JavaScript">
<!--HIDE
document.write("Buy my product")
document.write("<FONT SIZE='+3'>
→Now!</FONT>")
document.write("<FORM><INPUT TYPE='button'
→VALUE='Order'></FORM>")
//STOP HIDING-->
</SCRIPT>
</BODY>
</HTML>
```

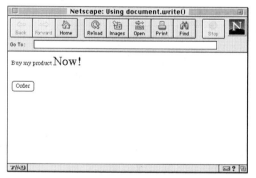

Figure 1.4 You can use document.write() to write HTML. This can range from unformatted text to components of the page.

WRITING HTML FROM JAVASCRIPT

You can use JavaScript to write HTML to a document. To accomplish this, you use **document.write()**, a basic command which adds the text and HTML within its parentheses to the current document.

As you learn more about JavaScript, you will see that you can use **document.write()** to customize an HTML document with user interaction.

To write text and HTML from a script:

> document.write("<FONT SIZE='+3'> Now!</FONT>")

1. document.write

Specify the name of the command you are using. In this case, type **document.write** to output to the HTML document.

2. (
)

Add parentheses after the command name. You will always include these when you are using a JavaScript command.

3. "<FONT SIZE=   >
Now!</FONT>"

Type the desired HTML within the parentheses. Surround it with quotation marks to differentiate it from JavaScript code.

4. '+3'

If you are writing an HTML tag that takes quotation marks, use single quotes in place of double quotes so JavaScript does not confuse the two.

WRITING PREFORMATTED TEXT

HTML normally ignores all formatting not specified in a tag. To display text exactly as you type it, you need to use either a preformatted text block or a dialog box.

When a script outputs text into a preformatted text block, you can make use of special JavaScript features to specify formatting. You will often want to break text onto a new line. You can do this in two ways, either with document.writeln() or by including the special character for a new line. In addition to this, JavaScript recognizes other special characters for several types of formatting, such as tabs and form feeds. Table 1.2 lists all of the special characters.

To write preformatted text:

> document.writeln("<PRE>o\r\t\tverand </PRE>")

1. document.writeln("
>   ")

Use **document.writeln()** to insert the specified content followed by a new line. This commands does the same thing as **document.write()**, except that it adds a line break.

2.   <PRE>

Signal the beginning of a preformatted text block with the preformatted tag.

3.   \r\t\t

Specify the special character or characters for the desired formatting. You can use the tab character to indent text and the return character to put it on a new line (see Figure 1.5).

4. </PRE>

Signal the end of the preformatted text block with the end-preformatted tag.

Script 1.5 Within the preformatted tag, document.writeln() adds a carriage return, while special characters allow for other formatting features. Here we've highlighted the special characters.

```
                        script
<HTML><HEAD>
<TITLE>Document.writeln() Example</TITLE>
</HEAD><BODY><SCRIPT LANGUAGE="JavaScript">
<!--HIDE
document.writeln("insunlightoverandoveringAonce
→uponatimenewspaper")
document.write("-eecummings")
document.writeln("<PRE>insu nli gh t\n\n\t\t
→o\r\t\tverand\r\t\to\r\t\tvering\n\nA\n\n\t\to
→nc\n\t\teup\n\t\tona\n\t\ttim\n\ne ne wsp
→aper")
document.write("-eecummings</PRE>")
//STOP HIDING-->
</SCRIPT>
</BODY></HTML>
```

Table 1.2 The special characters.

CHARACTER	WHAT IT MEANS
\f	form feed
\n	new line
\r	carriage return
\t	tab

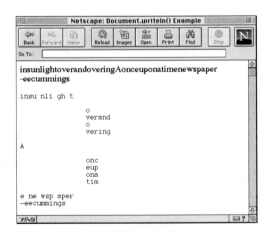

Figure 1.5 JavaScript's formatting features were introduced specifically so that it could display great poetry.

Script 1.5 Comments are used to include helpful information in your scripts.

```
                    script
<HTML>
<HEAD>
<TITLE>Comments Example</TITLE>
<SCRIPT LANGUAGE="JavaScript">
<!--HIDE
var name = "" //the user's name
/*This function uses a prompt to store
the user's name, and then welcomes her
by name.*/
function hello() {
    name = prompt("What is your name?","")
    alert("Welcome, " + name + ".")
}
//STOP HIDING-->
</SCRIPT>
</HEAD>
<BODY onLoad="hello()">
</BODY>
</HTML>
```

INSERTING COMMENTS IN A SCRIPT

Because languages like HTML and JavaScript try to evaluate all of the words in a document, you need to use special symbols to signal any text that you want them to ignore. This ignored text, called a *comment*, allows you to include information which may be useful to you or a reader in understanding the code. While not necessary to the functioning of the script, comments make your scripts easier to read and edit.

Script 1.5 shows the proper use of comments. It's okay if you don't understand how the script works, but you should examine the way the comments are used.

JavaScript includes two types of comments: single line and multiline. A single line comment tells the browser to ignore everything after it. Multiline comments mark off a block of code to be ignored.

To insert comments in a script:

/* comment */

1. /*

To create a comment which spans more than one line, signal its beginning with the open comment symbol. This tells the browser to ignore everything until the end of the comment.

OR //

To make the browser ignore the remainder of a line, you can use a double slash to indicate a single line comment. This makes the browser skip to the next line.

2. comment

Type the desired information. You should give brief descriptions of what the parts of your script do, as in Script 1.5.

3. */

Signal the end of the multi-line comment. This tells the browser to continue reading the script.

DISPLAYING AN ALERT MESSAGE

Dialog boxes provide a simple way to interact with the user. They can both display and receive information. JavaScript can create three types of dialog boxes: alert, prompt, and confirm. The following pages explain each of these.

All dialog boxes, like the buttons on a web page, use standard parts from the user's operating system. Because of this, an alert dialog box, for example, looks slightly different on a Macintosh than on a machine running Windows.

An alert dialog box is a standard dialog box with an alert icon and whatever text you specify. An OK button allows the user to clear the dialog box. You can display an alert dialog box with the alert command.

To display an alert message:

alert("message")

1. alert

Specify the alert command to display a simple dialog box like the one in Figure 1.6.

2. ( )

Include parentheses around your message. These signal JavaScript that you are invoking a command.

3. "message"

Type the desired message surrounded by quotation marks.

Script 1.6 The alert command creates a simple dialog box.

```
<HTML>
<HEAD><TITLE>Alert() Example</TITLE></HEAD>
<BODY>
<SCRIPT LANGUAGE="JavaScript">
<!--HIDE
alert("Welcome to my Web site!\nEnjoy your
→visit.")
//STOP HIDING-->
</SCRIPT>
</BODY>
</HTML>
```

Figure 1.6 An alert dialog box displays the message you specify. Special characters, such as new line (\n), can be used.

DISPLAYING AN ALERT MESSAGE

Script 1.7 A confirm dialog box allows you to ask the user questions.

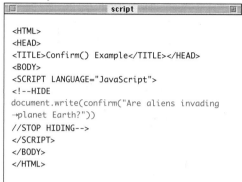

```
<HTML>
<HEAD>
<TITLE>Confirm() Example</TITLE></HEAD>
<BODY>
<SCRIPT LANGUAGE="JavaScript">
<!--HIDE
document.write(confirm("Are aliens invading
→planet Earth?"))
//STOP HIDING-->
</SCRIPT>
</BODY>
</HTML>
```

Figure 1.7 A confirm dialog box returns a true or false value.

DISPLAYING A CONFIRM DIALOG BOX

A confirm dialog box is exactly the same as an alert dialog box, except that it includes a second button (see Figure 1.7). In Windows the buttons are labeled OK and Cancel, on the Macintosh, Yes and No. The addition of the second button allows you to ask the user simple questions.

The confirm dialog box *returns* the user's answer to your script. This means that you can use the command name where you would type **true** or **false**. A confirm dialog box returns **true** if the user chooses OK and **false** if she chooses Cancel. You can generate confirm dialog boxs with the confirm command.

To display a confirm dialog box:

document.write(confirm("message"))

1.　　　　　　confirm(　　　　)

Use **confirm()** to display a dialog box with OK and Cancel buttons.

2.　　　　　　　　　"message"

Specify the text to be displayed in the dialog box surrounded by quotation marks.

3. document.write(　　　　　　　)

Because the confirm command returns **true** or **false**, your script can use this value. Putting **confirm()** within the parentheses of **document.write()** displays the user's response in the HTML page.

DISPLAYING A PROMPT DIALOG BOX

A prompt dialog box adds another component to the basic dialog box. It displays a text field in which the user can enter information (see Figure 1.8).

When the user clicks OK, whatever she has entered in the text field is returned to your script in place of the prompt command. This allows you to receive text input from the user.

Unlike the other commands you have seen, **prompt()** uses more than one item within its parentheses. These are called *arguments*, pieces of information that you give to the command. When there is more than one argument, you separate each with a comma. The prompt command's two arguments specify the message to display and the initial, or *default*, text which will appear in the text field.

To display a prompt dialog box:

document.write(prompt("message", ""))

1.   prompt(   )

Specify the prompt command followed by parentheses. You use the parentheses to hold its arguments.

2.   "message"

Specify the first argument, the message to display in the dialog box.

3.   ,""

Type a comma and then the second argument, the default text for the text field. You can type two quotation marks ("") to tell JavaScript to leave the field blank.

4. document.write(   )

Because **prompt()** returns the text entered by the user, you can display this in the page with **document.write()**, as in Figure 1.8.

Script 1.8 Prompt() accepts arguments for the message to display and default text.

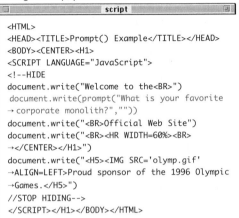

```
<HTML>
<HEAD><TITLE>Prompt() Example</TITLE></HEAD>
<BODY><CENTER><H1>
<SCRIPT LANGUAGE="JavaScript">
<!--HIDE
document.write("Welcome to the<BR>")
document.write(prompt("What is your favorite
→ corporate monolith?",""))
document.write("<BR>Official Web Site")
document.write("<BR><HR WIDTH=60%><BR>
→</CENTER></H1>")
document.write("<H5><IMG SRC='olymp.gif'
→ALIGN=LEFT>Proud sponsor of the 1996 Olympic
→Games.</H5>")
//STOP HIDING-->
</SCRIPT></H1></BODY></HTML>
```

Figure 1.8 The prompt dialog box allows the user to enter information.

DISPLAYING A PROMPT DIALOG BOX

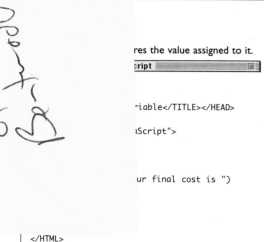

Sports

res the value assigned to it.

ript

riable</TITLE></HEAD>

Script">

ur final cost is ")

</HTML>

The keyword "var" alerts JavaScript that
you are defining a variable.

var myVariable

The name of your variable

Figure 1.9

VARIABLES

The pieces of information you work with in JavaScript, such as a message in a prompt command (see page 16), are called *values*.

By using quotation marks around a message, you signal that you are using a type of value called a *literal*, text that is typed directly into the script. This technique, however, greatly limits what you can do with this information. Not only will you need to retype this value to use it elsewhere in your script, but each message will be independent of the others. If your script performs an operation on one, the others will not change.

A *variable* solves this problem by storing a value. If you perform an operation on a variable, the value will change everywhere that you use it. Variables allow parts of your script to interact with one another.

You define a variable using the keyword **var**, as in Script 1.9. Once you have defined it, you can refer to your variable by the name you gave it. You should choose variable names according to the following rules.

Choosing a variable name:

1. **Use no spaces.** Instead, use the underscore character(_), or capitalize the first letter of each word after the first, as shown in Figure 1.9.

2. **JavaScript is case-sensitive.** This may be hard to get used to if you're accustomed to HTML. Standardize your naming procedure so you won't have to remember whether your variable name includes capitals.

3. **Make it original and descriptive.** It should be easy for you, or a user checking your script, to remember. Your variable names must also differ from the reserved words that are built into JavaScript.

WHAT ARE VARIABLES?

TYPES OF VALUES

Variables that store different types of information work in different ways. For example, it seems obvious that adding together two lines of text will do something different than adding together two numbers, but this is only possible because of JavaScript's use of *types*.

You can assign three types of values to variables: numbers, strings, and Booleans. JavaScript is a *loosely typed* language. This is a fancy way of saying that it doesn't really care what kind of value a variable stores. Because JavaScript is loosely-typed, you never need to tell it what type you are using, and you can change a variable's type at any time.

In order to understand how JavaScript works with information, you need to understand the three types of values.

String values:

Strings are sets of text. A string can be in the form of a literal that is specified in your script and surrounded with quotation marks. Strings can also be text entered by the user, such as in a prompt dialog box. When JavaScript requires a string, but you don't want any text to be displayed, you can use a *null string* ("").

Numerical values:

Numerical values are numbers. You can use them for mathematical operations.

Boolean values:

A Boolean value is either **true** or **false**. You usually generate a Boolean value by using a JavaScript command which returns one, such as **confirm()** (see page 15).

Figure 1.10 An error message tells you when a variable is not defined. Try to avoid these.

Script 1.10 A string variable can be used to store user input.

```
<HTML>
<HEAD><TITLE>String Example</TITLE></HEAD>
<BODY>
<H1>
<SCRIPT LANGUAGE="JavaScript">
<!--HIDE
var foo = prompt("Enter some text:")
document.write(foo)
//STOP HIDING-->
</SCRIPT>
</H1>
</BODY>
</HTML>
```

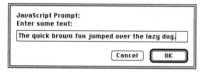

Figure 1.11 The user's text is stored in a variable and then output.

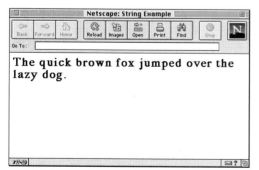

STORING TEXT AS STRINGS

JavaScript stores all text in the form of strings. Strings are essentially ordered sets of *characters*, which are individual letters, numbers, and symbols.

A variable that contains a string associates this text with a name. You create this association by assigning a value to the variable. You can do this with the *assignment operator*, the equals sign.

To tell JavaScript to treat text in your script as a string instead of a keyword, you must surround it with quotation marks.

To store text as a string:

1. var foo = prompt("Enter some text:")

var

Type the keyword **var** to tell JavaScript that you are creating a variable.

foo

Specify a name for your variable according to rules described on page 17.

=

Type an equals sign. This assignment operator associates a value with a variable.

prompt("Enter some text")

Because the prompt command returns the text the user has entered, you can use it to assign this string to a variable.

2. document.write(foo)

You access your variable by its name. By putting this in a **document.write()** you can output the value that you stored (see Figure 1.11).

STORING VALUES AS BOOLEANS

A Boolean has two possible values: **true** and **false**. Boolean variables allow you store a yes or no response generated by asking the user a question or by setting the response directly in your script. You can use Boolean variables to make simple decisions in your scripts, such as prompting the user to confirm an action.

Because **true** and **false** are Boolean values and not strings, you don't surround them with quotation marks. Instead, you assign a Boolean value simply by specifying one of these keywords.

To store a value as a Boolean:

1. var doYou

Declare a variable. This creates the variable, but does not give it a value or type.

2. doYou = confirm("Do you like eggy bread?")

doYou

Specify the name of your variable.

=

Use the assignment operator, the equals sign, to associate a value with your variable.

confirm("Do you like eggy bread?")

To store a user response, specify the confirm command and assign the value it returns to your variable.

3. document.write(doYou)

To output the value of the variable, specify it by name within a **document.write()** (see Figure 1.12).

Script 1.11 You can use a confirm dialog box to store a user's Boolean response in a variable.

```
<HTML>
<HEAD>
<TITLE>Assigning a Boolean Value</TITLE>
</HEAD>
<BODY><SCRIPT LANGUAGE="JavaScript">
<!--HIDE
var doYou
doYou = confirm("Do you like eggy bread?")
document.write("I'm told it is ")
document.write(doYou)
document.write(" that you like eggy bread.")
//STOP HIDING-->
</SCRIPT>
</BODY></HTML>
```

Figure 1.12 A confirm box asks an Englishman whether he likes French toast. The script then writes the resulting value to the document.

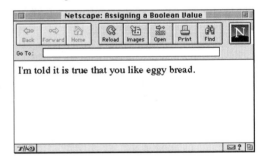

Script 1.12 You can assign a variable a number of octal, decimal, or hexadecimal base. Regardless of which base you use, JavaScript outputs in base 10.

```
                    script

<HTML>
<HEAD><TITLE>Numerical Values</TITLE>
</HEAD>
<BODY><SCRIPT LANGUAGE="JavaScript">
<!--HIDE
var myNumber = 652
var myNumberTwo = 0x28c
var myNumberThree = 6.52e2
alert(myNumber)
alert(myNumberTwo)
alert(myNumberThree)
//STOP HIDING-->
</SCRIPT></BODY>
</HTML>
```

NUMBER SYSTEM	SYNTAX
Decimal (base 10)	normal integer
Octal (base 8)	begin with 0
Hexadecimal (base 16)	begin with 0x

Table 1.3 Our everyday numbering system uses base 10. This means that the tenth digit in any column introduces a new column to the left. Computers often use octal or hexadecimal notation. These have 8 and 16, respectively, as their bases. In base 8 notation there can be no numeral higher than 7. Base 16 gets confusing because we only have ten numerals. This problem is solved by using the letters "a" through "f". Thus the number 46 (base 10) would be expressed as 2e in base 16.

STORING NUMBERS

Numerical variables store numbers. JavaScript can handle two types of numbers: integers and decimals. In programming, decimals are called *floating-point* numbers. You can specify them in either of two ways, as a decimal or using exponent notation.

You often need numbers in JavaScript for computer-related operations, and computers count differently than humans do. To control HTML color codes, for example, you need to work with hexadecimal numbers. You can use special syntax to specify a base as described in Table 1.3.

To store numbers:

1. var myNumber = 652

var myNumber

Declare a variable.

=

Use the assignment operator to associate a value with your variable.

652

Specify the number to store in the variable. To store a normal base 10 integer, simply type the number.

OR   0x28c

To store a hexadecimal number (base 16), prefix it with **0x**. You can use the letters **a** through **f** to represent numerals of 10 and beyond. **0x28c** is **652** in base 10.

OR   6.52e2

To store a decimal number, specify it in either normal decimal notation or exponent notation. In exponent notation, 652 is 6.52×10^2, or **6.52e2** in JavaScript.

2. alert(myNumber)

To ouput the number stored in a variable, specify it by name in a display command. JavaScript converts all numbers to base 10 before displaying them.

ARITHMETIC OPERATORS

To perform calculations with numbers in your script, you use special symbols called *operators*. These tell JavaScript how to change a value. For example, you use the addition operator to tell JavaScript to add the number on the right to the number on the left. These two numbers are called *operands*.

Basic math operators:

The basic math operators include addition, subtraction, multiplication and division. JavaScript uses the symbols in Table 1.4 to represent them.

The modulus operator:

Modulus refers to the remainder of a basic division operation. The modulus operator (%) returns the remainder of the left operand divided by the right operand.

Increment and decrement operators:

Increment (++) and decrement (--) simply add or subtract one from a single operand. If you place them before the operand they take effect immediately. If you place them after the operand, they don't take effect until after the current line, as illustrated in Script 1.13.

The negative operator

By placing a minus sign before a number or numerical variable you can reverse its sign.

Table 1.4 The arithmetic operators.

OPERATOR	WHAT IT DOES
+	adds the left and right operands
-	subtracts the right operand from the left
*	multiplies the operands
/	divides the left operand by the right
%	returns the remainder of the left operand divided by the right
++i	increments the operand by one
--i	decrements the operand by one
i++	increments the operand by one after the current expression
i--	decrements the operand by one after the current expression
-i	reverses the sign of the operand

Script 1.13 The final values of a and b are 99 and 100. The variable a is decreased by one only after its original value is assigned to b.

```
                       script
<HTML>
<HEAD>
<TITLE>Operators Example</TITLE></HEAD>
<BODY>
<PRE>
<SCRIPT>
<!--HIDE
var a = 100
var b = a--
document.writeln(a)
document.writeln(b)
//STOP HIDING-->
</SCRIPT>
</PRE>
</BODY>
</HTML>
```

ARITHMETIC OPERATORS

Script 1.14 You use the plus sign to combine multiple strings into one.

```
<HTML>
<HEAD>
<TITLE>Concatenating Strings</TITLE>
</HEAD>
<BODY>
<SCRIPT LANGUAGE="JavaScript">
<!--HIDE
var myString = "Java"
var myOtherString = "Script"
var combined = "This is a " + myString +
→myOtherString + " " + myOtherString + "."
alert(combined)
//STOP HIDING-->
</SCRIPT>
</BODY>
</HTML>
```

Figure 1.13 You can combine variables with spaces and punctuation to prepare them for display.

Combining Strings of Text

The addition operator has different effects in different contexts. If you use it with numbers it calculates their sum. When you use it with strings, however, it combines them into a single string.

This operation, called *concatenation*, converts any number of strings into one longer string. You will often want to concatenate variables with spaces and punctuation to display them in a format which is easy to read, as in Script 1.14.

To combine strings of text:

var combined = "text" + myString

1.   "text"

Designate the first string. You can use either variables or literals.

2.   +

Combine the two strings using a plus sign. This will create a larger string in which the last character of **myString** will be followed by the first character of your text.

3.   myString

Designate the second string.

4. var combined =

You can assign the new string to a variable for later use.

MODIFYING A VARIABLE

You have seen that you can assign value to a variable with the equals sign. This symbol belongs to a class of operators known as *assignment operators*, all used to assign value to variables. Because you will often need to modify a variable, the other assignment operators provide shortcuts for doing this. For example, if a variable stores the number **4** and you want to add **3** to it, you could type myVar = myVar + 3. You can use an assignment operator to abbreviate this as myVar += 3.

To modify a variable:

1. var theNumber = 4.11

Declare a variable and assign it the desired value with the equals sign.

2. theNumber *= 100

theNumber

Specify the variable to modify.

*=

Specify the desired assignment operator. An assignment operator consists of two parts: an operator and an equals sign. The times-equals operator, for example, assigns the product of the variable and the number you specify.

100

Enter the number to be used in the operation. This number would be the right operand if the statement were not abbreviated. Script 1.15 multiplies **theNumber** by **100** (see Figure 1.14).

Script 1.15 Assignment operators provide a shortcut to changing the value of a variable.

```
<HTML>
<HEAD><TITLE>Using Assignment Operators</TITLE>
</HEAD>
<BODY>
<SCRIPT LANGUAGE="JavaScript">
<!--HIDE
var a = "To reach"
a += " Information, dial "
var theNumber = 4.11
theNumber *= 100
document.write(a + theNumber)
//STOP HIDING-->
</SCRIPT>
</BODY>
</HTML>
```

Table 1.5 The assignment operators.

OPERATOR	WHAT IT MEANS
i = j	assigns the value of j to i
i += j	assigns the value of i + j to i
i -= j	assigns the value of i - j to i
i *= j	assigns the value of i * j to i
i /= j	assigns the value of i / j to i
i %= j	assigns the value of i % j to i

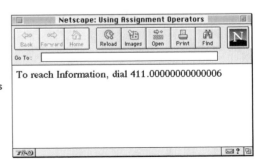

Figure 1.14 JavaScript displays sixteen places to the right of the decimal in a floating-point number. However, only the first thirteen of these are accurate. You can use the parsing functions in Chapter 6 to get around this problem.

OBJECTS AND EVENTS

Table 2.1 The computer as an object

QUALITIES	WHAT IT CAN DO
• Brand name	• Boot up
• Model name	• Run an application
• Processor type	• Perform math
• Processor speed	calculations
• Disk drive	• Shut down
(object)	

The concept of an object seems obvious. It is merely a thing, something that you can see or touch. But you can split this unit into two more basic categories: its qualities, and the things it can do.

If you think about a computer, for example, you can consider its attributes such as brand name and processor type, or its uses, such as running software and doing calculations.

You might consider your computer's disk drive an attribute, but you would also have to consider it an object in its own right. In this way, the attributes of a thing can also be objects.

JavaScript thinks along these same lines. In this chapter, you will learn how it works with objects, their qualities, and their uses.

OBJECT ORIENTATION

Many programming languages, Java and JavaScript among them, use objects to organize information. Programmers describe these languages as *object-oriented*.

The categories that you used to discuss a computer on the previous page are also the basic components of a JavaScript object. Its qualities, such as brand and model, are called its *properties*. The things it can do, such as run an application, are described as its *methods*.

To write HTML to a page, for example, you use document.write() (see page 11). In this piece of code, write() is a method belonging to an object called document. You use a period to address a property or method of an object. This system is called *dot syntax* (see Figure 2.1).

Object orientation has many advantages over procedural languages, which don't use this ordering system. Objects put related information and commands into logical groups, making them easier to work with. Document, for example, includes all the parts of a web document, from the links and images it includes to its background color.

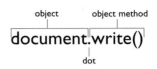

Figure 2.1 Dot syntax is used to address the properties and methods of objects.

THE OBJECT HIERARCHY

In full-fledged object-oriented programming languages, you have to create your own objects, but JavaScript includes just about every tool you need. Usually these objects correspond to tags in your HTML document.

JavaScript uses an object hierarchy to access and organize these parts of the page. The browser window, the object which contains all the others, sits at the top. This object has its own properties and methods. You treat any sub-object which falls inside of **window** as a property.

Sub-objects, like properties and methods, are associated with parent objects through dot syntax. These sub-objects can then have properties, methods, and sub-objects of their own.

To master JavaScript and address the parts of a page, you will need to learn its hierarchy. Figure 2.2 shows some of the levels of the object hierarchy. For a complete listing, see Appendix A.

Sometimes you will need to deal with information that has nothing to do with the page, such as the current date or a mathematical constant. JavaScript lets you do this through built-in objects, which are not part of the hierarchy. Table 2.2 provides a complete list of these. Unlike those in the hierarchy, you don't address built-in objects as sub-objects of window.

Table 2.2 These six objects are not parts of the page and therefore not sub-objects of the window.

BUILT-IN OBJECT	CONTAINS
Array	data indexed by name or number and methods for rearranging it
Date	current date, time, and time zone
Function	functions within script
Math	mathematical constants and functions
navigator	information about user's browser version, brand, and installed plug-ins
String	methods to work with text strings

THE OBJECT HIERARCHY

THE TOP LEVELS

The top most level in JavaScript's hierarchy is the browser window. This is addressed as **window**. Each window stores its current address in **location** and its previous URLs in **history**.

Within the window is the page the user is viewing. The contents of this page, including everything you define in HTML, comprise the third sub-object, **document**. The document includes all of the anchors, links, images, and forms on a page.

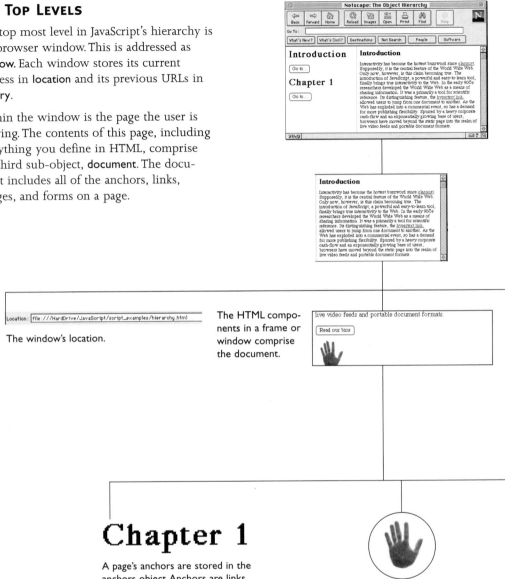

The window's location.

The HTML components in a frame or window comprise the document.

A page's anchors are stored in the anchors object. Anchors are links within a document.

A page's images are stored in the images object.

Figure 2.2 JavaScript organizes the objects you create with HTML in a hierarchy.

THE BROWSER HIERARCHY

THE LOWER LEVELS

Figure 2.2 depicts only the top four levels of JavaScript's object hierarchy. You can further subdivide each sub-object of **document** into multiple elements. For example, **forms[ ]** contains several elements, and each of these has its own properties.

All four objects in the fourth level store information as something called an *array*. JavaScript uses arrays to organize similar parts of the page in numerical order.

The images object, for example, contains all images on the page. To access a particular image, you need to type **images[ ]** and a number within the brackets.

JavaScript stores images and all array entries in the HTML order that they appear in your HTML. This order always begins with zero. You would refer to the first image on a page in code as **document.images[0]**, the second as **document.images[1]**, and so on.

At the top of the hierarchy is the window object. This represents all of the contents of the user's browser.

A window can contain multiple frames, which are stored in the frames object.

✓hierarchy.html	⌘0
CNN Interactive	⌘1
Welcome to Tripod: Tools For Life	⌘2
DARCY	⌘3
Toozeday Komix	⌘4
WORD	⌘5

The window's history.

Read our bios

A page's forms, each composed of buttons, text fields, and other elements, are stored in the forms object.

y a tool for scientif
he hypertext link,
nent to another. A

A page's hypertext links are stored in the links object.

ADDRESSING A FORM IN JAVASCRIPT

You can assign names to images, forms, and form elements (see Chapter 4) within your HTML tags. This makes it easier to refer to these objects in JavaScript using dot syntax (see page 26).

Assigning a form name in HTML:

`<FORM NAME="aForm">`

1. `<FORM        >`

Begin the form with the HTML form tag.

2. `    NAME`

Type **NAME**. You use this attribute in plain HTML with radio buttons and form submission, but you also use it for JavaScript addressing.

3. `       =`

Type the equals sign to signal assignment.

4. `      "aForm"`

Give your form a name.

Addressing a form in JavaScript:

document.forms[0]

1. document

Type **document** to begin the address.

2. `    .forms[ ]`

Use dot syntax to address the forms array. The braces signal that you are referring to an array.

3. `         0`

Give the index number of the form. **0** refers to the first form on the page.

OR document.aForm

Refer to the form by the name you have assigned in its HTML tag.

Script 2.1 Giving names to parts of your page makes it easier to refer to them in JavaScript.

```
script
<HTML>
<HEAD><TITLE>Naming Example</TITLE></HEAD>
<BODY>
<FORM NAME="aForm">
<INPUT TYPE="text">
</FORM>
<SCRIPT LANGUAGE="JavaScript">
<!--HIDE
document.write(document.aForm.name + "<BR>")
document.write(document.forms[0].name)
//STOP HIDING-->
</SCRIPT>
</BODY>
</HTML>
```

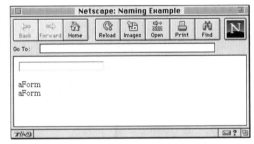

Figure 2.3 You can access the properties of an image, form, or form element with its name or array entry.

EVENTS AND EVENT HANDLERS

The user interacts with the parts of a web page through actions called *events*. You can use JavaScript to respond to events by using *event handlers*. JavaScript includes twelve event handlers, which are listed in Table 2.3.

You will generally want to trigger parts of your scripts with event handlers. A user clicks on a button; the JavaScript-enhanced page responds. You can accomplish this by assigning the desired response to **onClick** (Figure 2.4). Each part of the web page works with certain event handlers.

For the most part, the names of these event handlers describe when they work. A few, however, need explanation. Moving into a text field or window is called focusing, an event which triggers **onFocus**. Leaving a field or window triggers **onBlur**. If the user enters text before leaving a field, she triggers **onChange** but not **onBlur**.

Some events do not directly involve user actions. **OnError**, for example, triggers a response if the script encounters an error while running (see Chapter 7).

Table 2.3 The twelve event handlers

EVENT HANDLER	EVENT
onFocus	user moves focus to object
onBlur	user removes focus from object
onSelect	user highlights text
onChange	user changes value of object
onSubmit	user submits form
onClick	user clicks on button or link
onMouseOver	user moves cursor over link
onMouseOut	user moves cursor off link
onLoad	page or image finishes loading
onUnload	user leaves page
onAbort	user stops loading process
onError	script encounters error

Figure 2.4 The click events for the radio and button. You can trigger responses to these actions with event handlers.

RESPONDING TO EVENTS

Almost every part of a web page has at least one event handler. You can use these to make parts of the page trigger parts of your script.

By assigning a part of your script to an event handler, you tell JavaScript to read that part of the script when the event (what follows **on-**) occurs. You have to put the code you want to trigger within quotation marks.

To respond to an event:

<INPUT TYPE="text" onChange = "alert('Liar, Liar, Pants on Fire!')">

1. <INPUT TYPE="text"

>

Choose an HTML tag that you want to script.

2. onChange

Type the name of a relevant event handler after the HTML attributes. It should be all lowercase except for the letter after **on**.

3. =

Use the equals sign to signal assignment.

4. "alert('Liar, Liar, Pants on Fire!')"

Assign a response to the event by typing it after the equals sign and within quotation marks. Script 2.2 alerts the user with a message.

Script 2.2 You can use event handlers to trigger responses to user actions.

```
<HTML>
<HEAD><TITLE>Event Example</TITLE></HEAD>
<BODY>
Enter a lie:
<FORM>
<INPUT TYPE="text" onChange="alert('Liar, Liar,
→Pants on Fire!')">
</FORM>
</BODY>
</HTML>
```

Figure 2.5 Here an alert is triggered when the user changes the text and leaves the field.

Script 2.3 Here **this** is used to simplify the address of a form element.

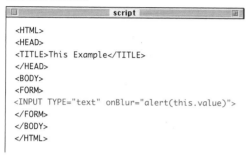

```
script
<HTML>
<HEAD>
<TITLE>This Example</TITLE>
</HEAD>
<BODY>
<FORM>
<INPUT TYPE="text" onBlur="alert(this.value)">
</FORM>
</BODY>
</HTML>
```

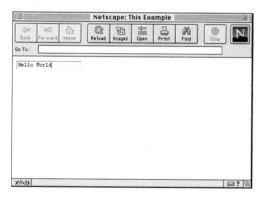

Figure 2.8 The keyword **this** simplifies addressing.

SHORTENING ADDRESSES WITH *THIS*

Sometimes JavaScript addresses can get rather long. For example, addressing the value of a text field requires at least four levels: **document.forms[0].elements[0].value**.

Fortunately, you can often shorten your addresses by using the keyword **this**. **This** stands in for the full object address. You should use **this** whenever possible to make your scripts clearer and more concise.

To shorten an address with *this*:

<INPUT TYPE="text" onBlur="alert (this.value)">

1. <INPUT TYPE="text" onBlur
>

Place an event handler within the desired HTML tag. Script 2.3 triggers an alert when the user tabs or clicks out of a text field.

2. ="alert
( )">

Assign a command to the event handler.

3. this

Type **this** to point the command to the object you are working with.

OR document.forms[0].elements[0]

If you don't use **this**, you have to type the complete address.

4. .value

Type a dot followed by the property you wish to access. Script 2.3 accesses the value of a field to display its text.

CREATING YOUR OWN OBJECT

As you saw on page 25, some JavaScript objects don't correspond to parts of the page. Unlike normal objects, you have to create instances of these objects to use them in your script. An instance is a single object, created from some common blueprint, called a constructor. When using **Date** (see Chapter 9), for example, your script could work with five different instances of this object, or none at all.

Table 2.4 shows the seven constructors you can use to create instances. Script 2.4 creates an empty object instance, which you can give properties and methods.

To create your own object:

1. var thingy = new Object()

var thingy =

Create a variable to store the new object instance by typing **var** and the name you want to give to the object. Type an equals sign to to assign value to your variable.

new

Type **new**. This tells JavaScript to create an object instance. JavaScript will make a copy of the blueprint that follows.

Object()

Type the name of the constructor that you want to use. **Object()** is an empty constructor. You have to fill it by assigning it properties and methods.

2. thingy.name = "thingamajigger"

Assign a property to your new object by following it with a dot, any word, and a value assignment. Basically, you can pretend that the property already exists. You do not need to declare it as a variable.

Script 2.4 You create instances with one of the constructors listed in Table 2.4.

```
<HTML>
<HEAD><TITLE>Creating Objects</TITLE>
<SCRIPT LANGUAGE="JavaScript">
<!--HIDE
var thingy = new Object()
thingy.name = "thingamajigger"
//STOP HIDING-->
</SCRIPT>
</HEAD><BODY>
<FORM>
<INPUT TYPE="button" VALUE="Show me!"
→onClick="alert(thingy.name)">
</FORM></BODY></HTML>
```

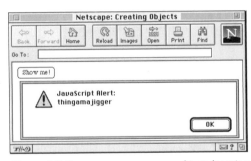

Figure 2.9 You can create your own objects by using the constructors.

Table 2.4 The seven constructors

CONSTRUCTORS	BLUEPRINT FOR
Array()	storing variables (see Chapter 10)
Date()	current date (see Chapter 9)
Function()	function (see Chapter 3)
Image()	image (see Chapter 8)
Option()	select list option (see Chapter 4)
String()	text string (see Chapter 6)
Object()	empty object

FUNCTIONS

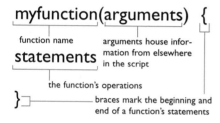

myfunction(arguments) {

function name

arguments house information from elsewhere in the script

statements

the function's operations

}

braces mark the beginning and end of a function's statements

Figure 3.1 You can group JavaScript commands into functions.

WHAT IS A FUNCTION?

You have seen that you can use JavaScript's methods to do simple things like display an alert or write to a document.

Often you will want to put together a group of methods to perform a more complex task. This group is called a *function*. When you create a function, you give a name to this set of commands. You can then trigger, or *call*, your function with this name.

For example, you have stored a user's response and then displayed it on the page. If you wanted to do this several times, you could repeat the same code. To be more efficient, however, you could put your code into a function and then call this function repeatedly.

DEFINING A FUNCTION

A function is a group of JavaScript statements with a name. You define the statements you want and the name you want for the group. Each time you call the function, JavaScript will read its commands in the sequence you typed them.

To define a function:

1. `<SCRIPT LANGUAGE="JavaScript">`

   Because you have to define a function before you can use it, place your script within the head tags to ensure that it is read first.

2. `function display()`

   function

   Type the keyword **function** to begin your definition.

   display

   Give your function a name. You should follow the same naming rules used for variables, which are listed on page 17.

   ()

   Add parentheses after the function name.

3. `{    alert("Have a Great Day!")    }`

   `{                              }`

   Mark the beginning and end of your function's statements with braces. As shown in Script 3.1, you should place the left brace after the function name and the right brace on its own line after all statements.

   `alert("Have a Great Day!")`

   Type the commands for your function to perform. For easier reading, you should tab these statements in from the rest of your script.

Script 3.1 You define your function's statements within braces.

```
script

<HTML>
<HEAD><TITLE>Function Example</TITLE>
<SCRIPT LANGUAGE="JavaScript">
<!--HIDE
function display() {
   alert("Have a Great Day!")
}
//STOP HIDING-->
</SCRIPT>
</HEAD>
<BODY>
Press Here for Important Information:
<FORM>
<INPUT TYPE="button" VALUE="Info" onClick=
→"display()">
<A HREF="#" onClick="display()">link</A>
</FORM></BODY></HTML>
```

Figure 3.2 You can use a function any number of times simply by calling it. Here user events trigger an annoying alert dialog.

Script 3.2 You can use an event handler to trigger a function call.

```
                         script
<HTML>
<HEAD><TITLE>Calling Example</TITLE>
<SCRIPT LANGUAGE="JavaScript">
<!--HIDE
function doMath() {
  var one = eval(document.theForm.
  →elements[0].value)
  var two = eval(document.theForm.
  →elements[1].value)
  var prod = one * two
  alert("The product of " + one + " and " +
  →two + " is " + prod + ".")
}
//STOP HIDING-->
</SCRIPT></HEAD>
<BODY><FORM NAME="theForm">Multiply
<INPUT TYPE="text"> by <INPUT TYPE="text">
<INPUT TYPE="button" VALUE="Show result"
→onClick="doMath()">
</FORM></BODY></HTML>
```

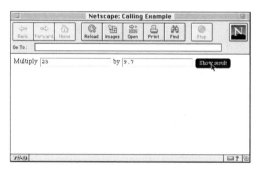

Figure 3.3 Here a button click triggers the function in Script 3.2.

CALLING A FUNCTION

Once you have defined a function, you can use it within any script or event handler on your page. Of course, to do this, you will need some way to trigger it. This is described as calling the function, and you can do it by typing the function's name followed by parentheses.

You can call a function any number of times, from almost anywhere on your page. You will usually use an event handler to trigger your function.

To call a function:

    <INPUT TYPE="button" VALUE="show result" onClick="doMath()">

1.   onClick="   "

To trigger your function with an event, place an event handler within an HTML tag. Script 3.2 uses a button for this purpose.

2.   doMath

Within the event handler, type the name of your function. Use the exact title you used in the function definition.

3.   ()

Add parentheses to the name to tell JavaScript that you are calling the function.

GIVING INFORMATION TO FUNCTIONS

You can't do very much with your functions if they are wholly self-contained. Because of this, you will often want to give them some information when you call them, such as the value of a text field. You can then use this information in the function's statements. When you give information to a function, it is called *passing* and the information you pass is called an *argument*.

An argument is basically a variable that JavaScript fills each time you call the function.

You will often pass the keyword **this** as an argument. By doing so you can easily refer to the calling object from within your function.

To give information to a function:

1. function doIt(theObject) {

function doIt   {

Define a name for your function.

(theObject)

Specify a name for your argument and surround it with parentheses. You use this name to refer to the value passed to the function. If you want your function to accept multiple arguments, separate them with commas.

2. <INPUT TYPE="text" onChange="doIt(this)">

doIt

Type the name of your function after an event handler and an equals sign.

( )

Add parentheses after the function name. You use these to contain the arguments you are passing.

this

Specify an argument. Script 3.3 passes **this** to a function to shorten references to a text field.

Script 3.3 You pass information to your functions in the form of arguments.

```
<HTML>
<HEAD>
<TITLE>Using Parameters</TITLE>
<SCRIPT LANGUAGE="JavaScript">
<!--HIDE
function doIt(theObject) {
    alert("I told you not to do that!")
    theObject.value="Don't Change this Info"
}
//STOP HIDING-->
</SCRIPT>
</HEAD>
<BODY>
<FORM>
<INPUT TYPE="text" VALUE="Don't Change Info"
→onChange="doIt(this)">
</BODY>
</HTML>
```

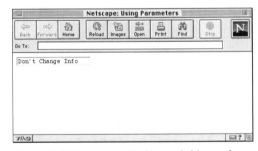

Figure 3.4 You can pass the keyword **this** to a function to make it easier to address objects.

Global Variables. Variables defined in the beginning of your script can be accessed anywhere on the page.

Local Variables. Both arguments and variables defined within a function are defined only while that function is running.

VARIABLE SCOPE

If you try to access an argument outside of its function, you'll get an error message saying that the variable is not defined. This is because arguments and variables that you define in a function only exist while that function is running.

Scope is what controls where your variables are defined. There are two kinds of scope: local and global.

So far you have worked only with variables that were *global* in scope. Because you declared them outside of any function, you could access them from anywhere on the page. If you declare a variable within a function, however, it is said to be *local* in scope. This means that outside of that function your script will not recognize the variable.

When convenient, you should try to use local variables instead of globals. Because they cease to exist when the function stops running, local variables do not waste memory. They also help you to avoid the confusion of using a single variable in multiple ways throughout your script.

When you do use them, you should define your global variables in the beginning of your script, before any functions.

USING A VALUE FROM A FUNCTION

You can use global variables to exchange information between parts of your script or you can write functions that return values. In this case, you can use the function call (**myFunction()**) as though it were a variable. JavaScript goes through the function, and then inserts the value it returns in place of its name.

To return a value you type the keyword **return** and the desired value or variable. You will normally want to make this statement the last line of your function's code, because it immediately stops the function.

To use a value from a function:

```
return item
```

1. return

Type the keyword **return** to signal that the function returns a value. You should put this at the end of your function, as in Script 3.4.

2.   item

Specify the value or variable that you wish to return. You can return any type of value, as well as global and local variables.

Script 3.4 To use a function's results in the script, end it with a return statement.

```
<HTML>
<HEAD><TITLE>Returning Values</TITLE>
<SCRIPT LANGUAGE="JavaScript">
<!--HIDE
function noReturn() {
   var unReturnedItem = 9*3
   }
function doReturn() {
   var item = 9*3
   return item
}
//STOP HIDING-->
</SCRIPT></HEAD>
<BODY>
<SCRIPT LANGUAGE="JavaScript">
<!--HIDE
document.write("Function noReturn yields " +
→noReturn())
document.write("<BR>Function doReturn yields "
→+ doReturn())
//STOP HIDING-->
</SCRIPT></BODY></HTML>
```

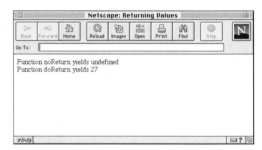

Figure noReturn yields undefined
Figure doReturn yields 27

Figure 3.5 Here a function defines a local variable and returns its value.

Script 3.5 By resetting an event handler, you can change the function called by a user event.

```
<HTML>
<HEAD>
<TITLE>Reset EventHandler Example</TITLE>
<SCRIPT LANGUAGE="JavaScript">
<!--HIDE
function shootOne() {
    alert("BANG!")
    document.links[0].onclick = shootTwo
}
function shootTwo() {
    alert("You're out of ammo. To reload the
    →gun, reload the page.")
}
//STOP HIDING-->
</SCRIPT></HEAD>
<BODY>
<A HREF="#" onClick="shootOne()">
<IMG SRC="gun.gif" NAME="gun" BORDER=0></A>
</BODY></HTML>
```

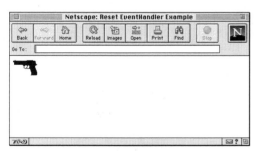

Figure 3.6 The user calls a different function by clicking on the gun the second time.

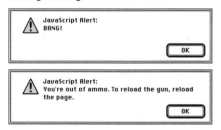

RESETTING EVENT HANDLERS

An event handler normally does the same thing each time it is triggered. This is usually not a problem. But what if you want a button to call one function the first time it is triggered and a different function if it is triggered again?

Navigator 3.0 solves this by allowing you to assign a new function to an event handler anywhere within your script. This technique is called resetting an event handler.

To reset an event handler, you need some way to address it within your script. You do this by addressing it as a property of the object it is associated with (see page 26).

To reset an event handler:

document.links[0].onclick = shootTwo

1. document.links[0]

Within a function, address the object that the event handler is associated with using dot syntax.

2. .onclick

Type a dot followed by the name of the event handler in all lowercase.

3. =

Use an equals sign to associate a new function with the event handler.

4. shootTwo

Specify the name of the new function. You must leave off the parentheses. If you include them JavaScript will call the function and assign the value it returns to the event handler. Remember, function calls use parentheses, but function references do not.

TRIGGERING FUNCTIONS WITH LINKS

Although you generally use event handlers to trigger a JavaScript function from within HTML, they can only respond to particular user actions. To allow greater flexibility, Netscape introduced two alternate ways to call functions. This page and the next discuss these techniques.

You can associate a JavaScript function with any link in an HTML document. You do this by assigning it to the HREF attribute.

To trigger a function with a link:

<A HREF="javascript:void(clammy())">

1. <A HREF=   >

Create an HTML link tag.

2.   "   "

Enclose your function call in quotation marks as if it were a URL.

3.   javascript:

Type **javascript** followed by a colon. This tells the browser to interpret the text as a JavaScript function instead of an HTML document.

4.   void(   )

Type **void** and then enclose your function call in parentheses. This ensures that the location of the page will not change when the function is called.

5.   clammy()

Specify the name of the function you want to call followed by parentheses.

Script 3.6 You can call a JavaScript function from any HTML link.

```
<HTML>
<HEAD><TITLE>Calling with a Link</TITLE>
<SCRIPT LANGUAGE="JavaScript">
<!--HIDE
function clammy(){
    var name = prompt("What's your first
    →name?", "")
    alert("Ugggggghhh, " + name + ", your hands
    →are clammy.")
}
//STOP HIDING-->
</SCRIPT></HEAD><BODY>
<CENTER><H1>Gimme some skin</H1>
<A HREF="javascript:void(clammy())">
<IMG SRC="hand.gif"></A></CENTER>
</BODY></HTML>
```

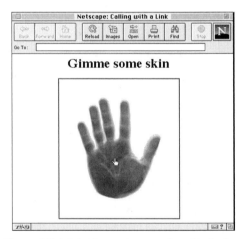

Figure 3.7 A link triggers the execution of a simple JavaScript function.

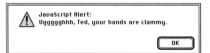

Script 3.7 JavaScript entities allow any expression to be used as an HTML value.

```
<HTML>
<HEAD><TITLE>Entities Example</TITLE>
<SCRIPT LANGUAGE="JavaScript">
<!--HIDE
function getWidth(){
  var w = eval(prompt("Enter image width:"))
  return w
}
function getHeight(){
  var h = eval(prompt("Enter image height:"))
  return h
}
//STOP HIDING-->
</SCRIPT></HEAD><BODY>
<CENTER><IMG SRC="hand.gif" WIDTH=
→"&{getWidth()};" HEIGHT="&{getHeight()};">
</CENTER></BODY></HTML>
```

Figure 3.8 Using JavaScript entities, an image can be scaled dynamically based on user input.

Assigning JavaScript to HTML

With Navigator 3.0, Netscape has expanded JavaScript's interaction with HTML. JavaScript *entities* are values from a script that you use in HTML. These allow your script to control what value is used for any HTML attribute. To do this, you just assign a JavaScript value surrounded by special characters to the attribute.

HTML uses entities for foreign letters and certain symbols. JavaScript uses the same characters (**&** and **;**), but requires that you surround your code with braces (**{}**).

To assign JavaScript code to an HTML attribute:

> <IMG SRC="hand.gif" WIDTH=
> "&{getWidth()};">

1.   WIDTH=

Within an HTML tag, type the attribute you wish to use followed by an equals sign. Script 3.7 uses JavaScript to determine an image source file.

2. &{

Type an ampersand followed by an open-brace to tell the browser that you are using a JavaScript entity.

3.   getWidth()

Specify a function or variable which returns an appropriate value. For example, if you are specifying an image width, as in Script 3.7, your function should return a number.

4.   };

Type a close-brace and semi-colon to end the entity.

CREATING A NEW FUNCTION

You normally think of a function as a grouping of JavaScript statements. However, the function is also an object in its own right.

Navigator 3.0 allows you to make new functions by treating them as objects. This technique involves declaring a new instance of the Function constructor (see page 34). Just as with a normal function definition, you tell JavaScript what you want to call the function and what statements it contains.

To create a new function:

var built = new Function(myCode)

1. var

Type the keyword **var** to tell JavaScript that you are creating a variable. This variable stores your function and acts as the function's name.

2. built

Give your function a name.

3. =

Use an equals sign to associate the new function with its name.

4. new

Type the keyword **new** to signal that you are creating an instance of a constructor.

5. Function

Specify that you are using the Function constructor.

6. (myCode)

Within parentheses, type the statements for your function or the name of a variable that contains them.

Script 3.8 The Function constructor provides a different way to define functions.

```
<HTML>
<HEAD><TITLE>Function Example</TITLE>
<SCRIPT LANGUAGE="JavaScript">
<!--HIDE
function make(myCode) {
    var built = new Function(myCode)
}
//STOP HIDING-->
</SCRIPT></HEAD>
<BODY>
<H1>Enter the code for a new function:</H1>
<FORM>
<TEXTAREA ROWS=5 COLS=40>
</TEXTAREA>
<BR>
<INPUT TYPE="button" VALUE="define function"
→onClick="make(this.form.elements[0].value)">
<INPUT TYPE="button" VALUE="run function"
→onClick="built()">
</FORM></BODY></HTML>
```

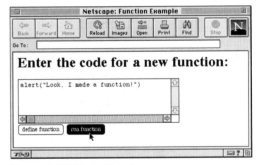

Figure 3.9 With the Function constructor, you can create a function from text entered by the user.

Script 3.9 The caller property can refer to an event handler or function.

```
<HTML>
<HEAD><TITLE>Caller Example</TITLE>
<SCRIPT LANGUAGE="JavaScript">
<!--HIDE
function two() {
   message()
}
function message() {
   alert("This alert function was called by " +
   →message.caller)
   document.forms[0].elements[0].onclick=two
}
//STOP HIDING-->
</SCRIPT></HEAD>
<BODY>
<FORM>
<INPUT type="button" Value="click me"
→onClick="message()"
</FORM></BODY></HTML>
```

Figure 3.10 The caller property reads an event handler as a function.

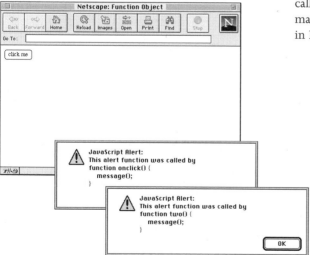

DETERMINING A FUNCTION'S TRIGGER

When an event handler or function calls another function (see page 37), it is known as the *caller*. You can use this information combined with the tools described in Chapter 5 to make your function do different things depending, for example, on which button called it.

To get this information you use the caller property of your function.

To determine what triggered a function:

> alert("This alert function was called by " + message.caller)

1. message

Within a display command, type the name of your function. This addresses it as an object.

2.   .caller

Specify the caller property. **Caller** stores the code of the function's caller as a string. This string includes the full text of the function or event handler. If the caller is an event handler, JavaScript formats the string like a function, as shown in Figure 3.10.

USING EXTRA ARGUMENTS

You normally pass a function the same number of arguments as you declare in its definition. If you pass it more than this you won't get an error, but you won't be able to refer to the extras.

You can get around this limitation using your function's arguments array. **Arguments[ ]** stores each value that was passed to the function. You can use this information to create a function that can work with any number of arguments.

To use extra arguments:

1. function putTogether(greet) {

Define your function. The one in Script 3.10 declares only one argument.

2. var args = putTogether.arguments.length

putTogether.arguments.length

Type the name of your function followed by **.arguments.length** to determine how many arguments there are.

var args =

You can store the length of the arguments array and use it later.

3. greet += " " + putTogether.arguments[i]

Use a for loop (discussed in Chapter 5) to do something with each entry in the arguments array. Script 3.10, for example, concatenates all of the values into a single string. You access the extra arguments by their index number in the array.

4. putTogether(theForm.one.value,theForm.two .value,theForm.three.value)

Pass your function the desired values. You can pass as many as you want, because your function uses the arguments array.

Script 3.10 The arguments array stores all of the values passed to a function.

```
<HTML>
<HEAD><TITLE>Arguments Example</TITLE>
<SCRIPT LANGUAGE="JavaScript">
<!--HIDE
function putTogether(greet) {
    var args = putTogether.arguments.length
    for(var i=1; i<args; ++i) {
        greet += " " + putTogether.arguments[i]
    }
    document.theForm.output.value = greet
}
//STOP HIDING-->
</SCRIPT></HEAD>
<BODY><FORM NAME="theForm">
<INPUT TYPE="text" NAME="one">
<INPUT TYPE="text" NAME="two">
<INPUT TYPE="text" NAME="three">
<INPUT TYPE="button" VALUE="greet me"
onClick="putTogether(theForm.one.value,theForm.
→two.value,theForm.three.value)">
<BR><BR>GREETING: <INPUT TYPE="text" NAME="out-
put" SIZE=52></FORM></BODY></HTML>
```

Figure 3.11 The arguments array allows you to repeat a procedure for any number of arguments.

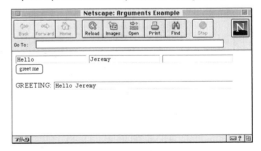

WORKING
WITH FORMS

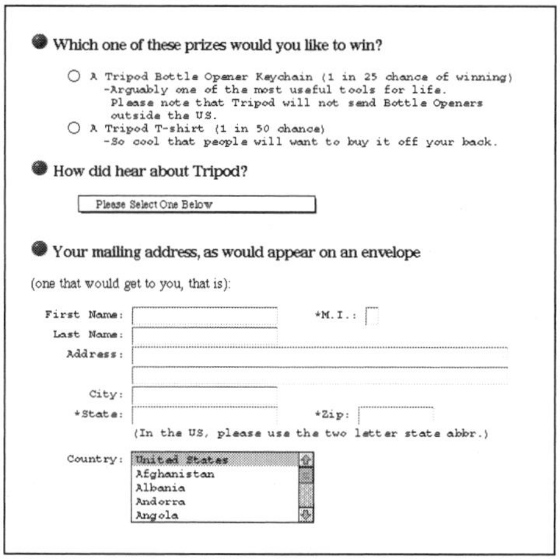

Figure 4.1 You can use the elements of a form to trigger parts of your script.

Every web user has used a form at one time or another. You enter some information and click a submit button to send it to the server. With JavaScript, your page can work with this input immediately instead of waiting for the server.

JavaScript stores each form on your page as an entry in **forms[ ]**.

Within each pair of form tags, you define the buttons, text fields, and other elements that you want to include in the form. JavaScripts stores each of these elements within **elements[ ]**, an array which you can access for each form.

In this chapter, you will learn how to use JavaScript with forms and form elements. By inserting event handlers (see Chapter 2) in your element tags, you can use elements to trigger parts of your script.

RESPONDING TO A BUTTON CLICK

HTML allows you to create a button that looks like a submit or reset button but accomplishes nothing unless it is scripted. By using **onClick**, you can make this button trigger parts of your script.

You will use buttons frequently as you go through the examples in this book. Table 4.1 explains the properties of the button object. We will use these tables throughout the rest of the book to tell you the event handlers, properties, and methods associated with an object.

To respond to a button click:

```
<INPUT TYPE="button" NAME="meenie"
VALUE="Meenie" onClick="thanks(this)">
```

1. `<INPUT TYPE="button"`

   `>`

   Type ="button" after **INPUT TYPE** to create a button element.

2. `NAME="meenie"`

   Type **NAME=** and the name you want to give your button in quotation marks. Once you have assigned a value to the name attribute, you can address your button in JavaScript through this name.

3. `VALUE="Meenie"`

   Type **VALUE=** and the text that you want to display in the button.

4. `onClick`

   Use **onClick** to trigger a part of your script when the user clicks on the button.

5. `="thanks(this)">`

   Assign to **onClick** the name of the function you want to trigger, followed by parentheses. Script 4.1 passes **this** to thanks(), so that the function can work with the button object.

Table 4.1

button object	Click!

PROPERTIES	EVENT HANDLERS
name value of name attribute	onClick user clicks on button
value text shown in button	

Script 4.1 You can use a button click to trigger a part of your script.

```
<HTML>
<HEAD><SCRIPT LANGUAGE="JavaScript">
<!--HIDE
function thanks(theButton) {
    alert("Thank you for clicking on " +
    →theButton.value + ".")
}
//STOP HIDING--></SCRIPT>
<BODY><FORM>
<INPUT TYPE="button" NAME="eenie" VALUE="Eenie"
→onClick="thanks(this)">
<INPUT TYPE="button" NAME="meenie"
→VALUE="Meenie" onClick="thanks(this)">
<INPUT TYPE="button" NAME="miney" VALUE="Miney"
onClick= "thanks(this)">
</FORM></BODY></HTML>
```

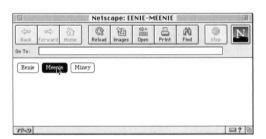

Figure 4.2 When the user clicks a button, she triggers an alert that displays the button's value.

Table 4.2

radio object	
PROPERTIES	**EVENT HANDLERS**
checked true if selected	onClick user clicks on radio
defaultChecked true if selected by default	
index array of buttons	
length number of buttons	
name value of name attribute	
value value of value attribute	

Script 4.2 Checked stores **true** if a radio button is selected, false if it is not.

```
script
<HTML><HEAD>
<SCRIPT LANGUAGE="JavaScript">
<!--HIDE
function tellMe(theForm) {
  alert(theForm.group[0].checked)
}
//STOP HIDING-->
</SCRIPT></HEAD>
<BODY><FORM>
<INPUT TYPE="radio" NAME="group" CHECKED>
Choice 1<BR>
<INPUT TYPE="radio" NAME="group">Choice 2<BR>
<INPUT TYPE="radio" NAME="group">Choice 3<BR>
<INPUT TYPE="button" VALUE="Choice 1 is
→Selected." onClick="tellMe(this.form)">
</FORM>
</BODY></HTML>
```

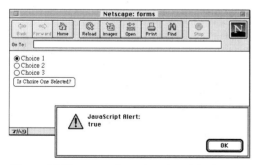

Figure 4.3 This script alerts the value of the first button's checked property.

WORKING WITH RADIO BUTTONS

You use radio buttons in HTML like a select list. In each case, the user can only make one selection. Your script can work with the properties listed in Table 4.2. By checking whether a radio button is selected, your script can make decisions about what it will do next (see Chapter 5).

To determine if a radio button is checked:

1. function tellMe(theForm) {

Define a function that accepts one argument (see page 38). The argument will store a reference to the form.

2. alert(theForm.group[0].checked) }

    alert(**)** }

Put an alert message within this function.

      theForm

Tell JavaScript which form you are accessing by specifying the argument.

        .group

Type a dot and then the name of your radio buttons.

      [0]

Within brackets, specify the index number of the radio button you want to test. Script 4.2 uses **0** to determine whether the first radio button is checked.

        .checked

Type a dot and then **checked** to access this property of the radio button. **Checked** stores **true** if the button is checked and **false** if it is not.

3. onClick="tellMe(this.form)"

Within an HTML button tag, assign your function to **onClick**. Pass it **this.form** so it can address the correct form with just one word.

SELECTING A RADIO BUTTON

Usually, you'll want the user to control which radio button is checked, but you can also make this selection through your script. You might want to do this to update information as the user progresses through the form.

To select a radio button:

1. function change(num) {

Define a function with one argument (see page 38), which will store the number of the radio button to select.

2. document.forms[0].rad[num].checked = true}

document.forms[0].rad

Within this function, type the address of the radio buttons.

[num]

Within brackets, type the name of your function's argument.

.checked

Type **.checked** to address the button's checked property.

= true

Assign **true** to this property to select the radio button. You can assign **false** to de-select it.

3. onClick="change(2)"

onClick="change   "

In each radio HTML tag, assign your function to **onClick**.

(2)

Type the index number of the radio button you want to select in parentheses. Script 4.3 changes the user's selection by passing the number of a different button.

Script 4.3 Using the checked property, you can select of a radio button through your script.

```
<HTML>
<HEAD>
<SCRIPT LANGUAGE="JavaScript">
<!--HIDE
function change(num) {
    document.forms[0].rad[num].checked = true
}
//STOP HIDING-->
</SCRIPT></HEAD>
<BODY><FORM>
<INPUT TYPE="radio" NAME="rad" VALUE="one"
→CHECKED onClick="change(1)">
<INPUT TYPE="radio" NAME="rad" VALUE="two"
→onClick="change(2)">
<INPUT TYPE="radio" NAME="rad" VALUE="three"
→onClick="change(0)">
</FORM></BODY>
</HTML>
```

Figure 4.4 Think of it as a sort of no-win 3-card monte. When the user selects one radio button, the script selects another.

Table 4.3

checkbox object	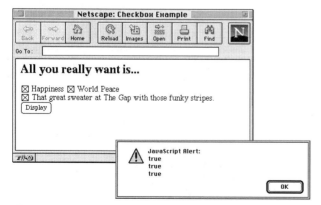

PROPERTIES	METHODS
checked true if selected	click() selects a checkbox
defaultChecked true if selected by default	
	EVENT HANDLERS
name value of name attribute	onClick user selects checkbox
value value of value attribute	

Script 4.4 Checked stores true if the checkbox is checked and false if it is not.

```
<HTML>
<HEAD><TITLE>Checkbox Example</TITLE>
<SCRIPT LANGUAGE="JavaScript">
<!--HIDE
function display() {
    alert(document.forms[0].one.checked + "\n" +
    →document.forms[0].two.checked + "\n" +
    →document.forms[0].three.checked)
}
//STOP HIDING-->
</SCRIPT></HEAD>
<BODY>
<H2>All you really want is...</H2>
<FORM>
<INPUT TYPE="checkbox" NAME="one">Happiness
<INPUT TYPE="checkbox" NAME="two">World Peace
<INPUT TYPE="checkbox" NAME="three">That great
→sweater at The Gap with those funky stripes.
<INPUT TYPE="button" VALUE="Display"
→onClick="display()">
</FORM></BODY></HTML>
```

WORKING WITH CHECKBOXES

You use checkboxes in HTML so that the user can make one selection without affecting the others. Table 4.3 lists the parts of a checkbox that you can work with in JavaScript. Script 4.4 works with the checked property.

To determine if checkboxes are selected:

1. alert(document.forms[0].one.checked)

    document.forms[0].one

Within your display function, address the desired checkbox.

    .checked

Follow this with **.checked**. If the box is checked, this stores **true**, if not, it stores **false**.

alert(   )

Display this information by putting it within an alert command.

2. onClick="display()"

Within the desired HTML tag, assign your display function to an event handler (see page 37).

Figure 4.5 For cases where the user just can't make up his mind, a checkbox allows for multiple choices.

CHANGING TEXT FIELDS

The text field is the most important part of an interactive web page. The user can give your script information through it or your script can display information. JavaScript treats anything the user types into a text field as a string called **value**.

You can work with the parts of a text field listed in Table 4.4.

To change the text in a text field:

1. function doIt(theForm) {

Define a function with one argument (see page 38), a reference to the text field's form.

2. theForm.text2.value = theForm.text1.value

theForm.text2

Within this function, type the argument. Add a dot and the name or **elements[ ]** address of the text field you want to change.

.value

Address this field's text. This stores whatever text is in the text field.

= theForm.text1.value

Assign a new string to the text field with the equals sign. Script 4.5 copies the words from one text field into another.

3. onBlur = doIt(this.form)

onBlur = doIt

Trigger your function with an event handler by placing it in the desired HTML tag (see page 37). Script 4.5 copies the text as soon as the user leaves the first text field.

(this.form)

Pass your function **this.form**, so that it can address the form you are using with only one word (see page 33).

Table 4.4

text object	My text

PROPERTIES	EVENT HANDLERS
name value of name attribute	onFocus user focuses on field
value text within field	onBlur user leaves field
defaultValue initial text	onChange user changes text and leaves field
METHODS	
focus() jump to a text field	onSelect user selects text
blur() leave a text field	
select() select all text	

Script 4.5 Blurring out of the first text fields copies its contents to the second.

```
<HTML>
<HEAD><TITLE>Text Input</TITLE>
<SCRIPT LANGUAGE="JavaScript">
<!--HIDE
function doIt(theForm) {
    theForm.text2.value = theForm.text1.value
}
//STOP HIDING-->
</SCRIPT></HEAD>
<BODY><FORM>
<INPUT TYPE="text" NAME="text1" VALUE="Enter
→text" onBlur="doIt(this.form)">
<INPUT TYPE="text" NAME="text2">
</FORM></BODY></HTML>
```

Figure 4.6 This script copies the user's text to a second field.

Script 4.6 By blurring a field when the user clicks on it, you can ensure that the doesn't write in it.

```
                    script
<HTML>
<HEAD><TITLE>Uneditable Text Block</TITLE>
<SCRIPT LANGUAGE="JavaScript">
<!--HIDE
function doIt() {
   document.forms[0].disp.value = "Hi " +
   ⇥document.forms[0].elements[0].value + " " +
   ⇥document.forms[0].elements[1].value + "!"
}
//STOP HIDING-->
</SCRIPT></HEAD>
<BODY><FORM>
<INPUT TYPE="text" VALUE="first name"><BR>
<INPUT TYPE="text" VALUE="last name"><BR>
<TEXTAREA onFocus="blur()">Display</TEXTAREA>
<BR>
<INPUT TYPE="button" VALUE="Evaluate"
⇥onClick=doIt()>
</FORM></BODY></HTML>
```

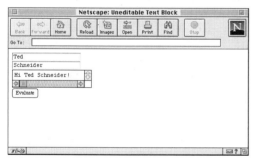

Figure 4.7 You can use a text field to display text to the user.

USING TEXT FIELDS FOR DISPLAY

You'll often want to use a text field to display information to the user. You should choose this technique over an alert if you will be displaying lots of information or you don't want to annoy the user with a dialog box.

It would be nice if JavaScript could use a separate part of the page for displaying text, but no such form element exists in HTML. Instead, you can adapt a normal text field so that the user cannot enter it.

To display information in a text field:

1. document.forms[0].disp.value = "Hi "

   Within a function, display the desired message by assigning it to the value of the text field.

2. <TEXTAREA onFocus="blur()">Display </TEXTAREA>

   <TEXTAREA   >Display </TEXTAREA>

   Type the HTML tags for either a text field or text block.

   onFocus

   Type **onFocus** to trigger an event when the user tabs or clicks into the text box.

   ="blur()"

   Assign **blur()** to **OnFocus** with an equals sign. As soon as the user moves into the text box, JavaScript will move him out, as in Script 4.6.

WORKING WITH MENU ITEMS

You create menus in HTML by using the select and option tags. As shown in Table 4.5, JavaScript includes many properties to work with both of these.

A select menu includes a number of options. JavaScript treats each of these options as a sub-object. You can access each item in the menu through options[ ].

To use a selected menu item in a function:

1. function display(selector) {

Define a function with one argument (see page 38), a reference to the select list.

2. selector.options[selector.selectedIndex].text

selector.options[   ]

Wherever you want to use the selected menu item in your function, type the argument and then **.options[ ]**. This addresses the options array of your menu.

selector.selectedIndex

Type the name of your argument and **.selectedIndex** within the brackets. Because **selectedIndex** stores the number of the currently selected item, you can use it to address this item.

.text

Type a dot followed by **text** to access the the text of the selected menu item. Script 4.7 displays this information in a text field.

3. onChange="display(this)"

Trigger your function with an event handler in an HTML tag. Script 4.7 passes the function **this** to make the menu easier to address (see page 33).

Table 4.5

select object	Option 1

PROPERTIES	**METHODS**
length number of options	blur() deactivates list
name value of name attribute	focus() activates list
options array of options	**EVENT HANDLERS**
selectedIndex index of selected option	onFocus user clicks on list
PROPERTIES OF OPTIONS	onBlur user leaves list
defaultSelected initial option	onChange user changes option
index index of current option	
length number of options	
name value of name attribute	
selected true if selected	
selectedIndex selected option	
text text displayed in list	
value value of value attribute	

Script 4.7 selectedIndex stores the index number of the selected menu item.

```
script
<HTML><HEAD><TITLE>Select Example</TITLE>
<SCRIPT LANGUAGE="JavaScript">
<!--HIDE
function display(selector) {
   selector.form.field.value= "So, you want to
   →order " + selector.options[selector.
   →selectedIndex].text + "."
}
//STOP HIDING--></SCRIPT></HEAD><BODY><FORM>
<H2>I would like to order
<SELECT NAME="order" onChange="display(this)">
<OPTION>100 JavaScript T-shirts
<OPTION SELECTED>50 copies of your book
<OPTION>a lifesize poster of Ted and Jeremy
<OPTION>everything you've got
</SELECT><BR>
<INPUT TYPE="text" SIZE=60 name="field">
</H2></FORM></BODY></HTML>
```

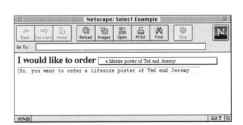

Figure 4.8 A message to the user includes the text of the selected menu item.

Script 4.8 You can change the text of any item in a pull-down menu.

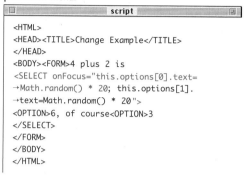

```
<HTML>
<HEAD><TITLE>Change Example</TITLE>
</HEAD>
<BODY><FORM>4 plus 2 is
<SELECT onFocus="this.options[0].text=
→Math.random() * 20; this.options[1].
→text=Math.random() * 20">
<OPTION>6, of course<OPTION>3
</SELECT>
</FORM>
</BODY>
</HTML>
```

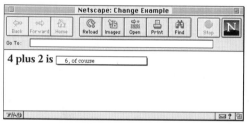

Figure 4.9 When the user tries to choose the obvious answer, a new set of entries appears.

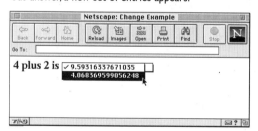

Changing Menu Item Text

You can use JavaScript to change the text of any menu item. You might want to do this to update a menu with information the user enters elsewhere in a form.

To change the text of a menu item:

> <SELECT onFocus="this.options[0].text = Math.random() * 20">

1. **<SELECT onFocus=" ">**

   Within the menu's select tag, insert the onFocus event handler to respond to the user's entry.

2. **this**

   Type **this** to address the select menu.

3. **.options**

   Type **.options** to address the options array.

4. **[0]**

   Specify the index number of the option you wish to change within brackets.

5. **.text**

   Address the text displayed for this option.

6. **= Math.random() * 20**

   Assign your new value to the option. Script 4.8 replaces the menu item with randomly generated numbers (see Chapter 6).

CHANGING MENU ITEM SELECTIONS

JavaScript allows you to determine which item in your menu is selected. In a normal HTML menu, the user and your script can only select one item. If your HTML select tag includes the multiple attribute, however, both your script and the user can select multiple items.

To change which menu item is selected:

onClick="this.form.order.selectedIndex = 0"

1. onClick="   "

Use an event handler within an HTML tag so that a user action triggers the menu change (see page 32). Script 4.9 accesses a select list from a radio button.

2.   this.form.order

Type the address of your select list.

3.   .selectedIndex = 0

Type .selectedIndex = and the index number of the option you want to select.

CHANGING WHICH MENU ITEM IS SELECTED

Script 4.9 Depending on the type of menu you have created in HTML, you can select items through selectedIndex and options[ ].selected.

```
<HTML>
<HEAD><TITLE>Selecting Example</TITLE></HEAD>
<BODY><FORM>
<H2>My favorite berry is:<BR>
<INPUT TYPE="radio" NAME="fruit"
→onClick="this.form.order.selectedIndex = 0">
strawberry<BR>
<INPUT TYPE="radio" NAME="fruit"
→onClick="this.form.order.selectedIndex = 1">
blueberry<BR>
<INPUT TYPE="radio" NAME="fruit"
→onClick="this.form.order.selectedIndex = 2">
Berry Berry Kix<BR><BR>
To order <SELECT NAME="order" MULTIPLE
→onFocus="blur(this)">
<OPTION>100 lbs. strawberries
<OPTION>100 lbs. blueberries
<OPTION>a box of cereal</SELECT>
<INPUT TYPE="button" VALUE="click here.">
</H2></FORM></BODY></HTML>
```

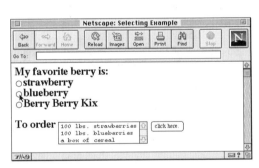

Figure 4.10 You can change the default menu selection based on user input.

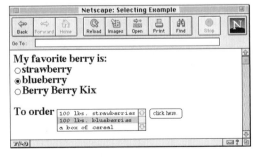

Script 4.10 You can generate an entirely new menu item with the option constructor.

```
<HTML>
<HEAD><TITLE>Option Constructor Example</TITLE>
<SCRIPT LANGUAGE="JavaScript">
<!--HIDE
function newItem() {
   var d = new Option("everything you've got")
   document.forms[0].order.options[3]=d
}
//STOP HIDING-->
</SCRIPT></HEAD>
<BODY><FORM>
<H2>I would like to order
<SELECT NAME="order">
<OPTION>100 JavaScript T-shirts
<OPTION SELECTED>50 copies of your book
<OPTION>a lifesize poster of Ted and Jeremy
</SELECT><BR>
<INPUT TYPE="button" VALUE="I would appreciate
→more choices." onClick="newItem()">
</H2></FORM></BODY></HTML>
```

✓ 100 JavaScript T-shirts
   50 copies of your book
   a lifesize poster of Ted and Jeremy

Figure 4.11 The option created with the constructor appears instantly on the selection list.

✓ 100 JavaScript T-shirts
   50 copies of your book
   a lifesize poster of Ted and Jeremy
   everything you've got

ADDING NEW MENU ITEMS

In addition to changing what a menu item says, you can add an entirely new one, as we've done in Script 4.10. To do this you create an instance of the Option constructor (see page 34).

When you build an option in JavaScript you specify all the attributes you would have given it in HTML. Once you've created the option you can add it to the menu.

To add a new menu item:

1. var d = new Option("everything you've got")

> **new**

Within a function type **new** to create an object instance.

> Option(   )

Specify the Option constructor to create a new item for a menu.

> "everything you've got"

Type the text for the new option within quotation marks.

> var d =

Assign all of this to a new variable so that you can address it.

2. document.forms[0].order.options[3] = d

document.forms[0].order.options[ ]

Within the same function, address the array of menu items (see page 54).

> 3

Address an empty entry in **options[ ]**. The index number should be one more than that of the last menu item in your HTML.

> = d

Type the equals sign and your variable to add your new option to the menu.

HIDDEN ELEMENTS

Unlike the other form elements, the hidden object isn't visible. But when the user submits a form, the hidden object goes with it. You can use the hidden element to send information to the server that you don't want the user to see.

When working with multiple windows (see Chapter 10), you can use the hidden object to make a form that spans multiple pages. You use it any time you want to pass information from one form to another.

To pass information from one form to another:

1. <INPUT TYPE="hidden" NAME="hider">

Create two HTML forms, as in Script 4.10. Within the second, define a hidden element. You can name it to address it more easily.

2. document.forms[1].hider.value
= document.forms[0].elements[0].value

document.forms[1].hider.value

Within a function in your script, address the value of the hidden object in the second form.

= document.forms[0].elements[0].value

Type an equals sign and the address of the property in the first form that you want to copy to the second. See page 26 for information on addressing.

3. onChange="changer()"

Trigger your function with onChange in the text field you want to copy (see page 32). When the user changes this text and tabs out of the field, it will be passed to the hidden object in the second form.

Script 4.10 You use the hidden object to pass information from one form to another.

```
<HTML>
<HEAD><TITLE>Hidden Object Example</TITLE>
<SCRIPT LANGUAGE="JavaScript">
<!--HIDE
function changer() {
    document.forms[1].hider.value =
    →document.forms[0].elements[0].value + ";" +
    →document.forms[0].elements[1].value
}
//STOP HIDING--></SCRIPT></HEAD>
<BODY><FORM ACTION=".//maillist">
<H2>Sign up for our mail-list:<BR>
Name:<INPUT TYPE="text">
email:<INPUT TYPE="text" onChange="changer()">
</H2>
<INPUT TYPE="submit" VALUE="Send
it!"></FORM><HR>
<FORM ACTION=".//order">
<H2>Order our goods:<BR>
Product:<INPUT TYPE="text">
Quantity:<INPUT TYPE="text"></H2>
<INPUT TYPE="hidden" NAME="hider">
<INPUT TYPE="submit" VALUE="Send it!"></FORM>
</BODY></HTML>
```

Figure 4.12 Sending the second form includes the information in the first, which is stored in the hidden object.

Script 4.11 The reset button can be scripted to give the user a second chance.

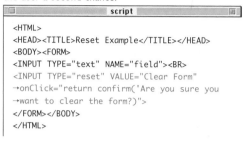

```
<HTML>
<HEAD><TITLE>Reset Example</TITLE></HEAD>
<BODY><FORM>
<INPUT TYPE="text" NAME="field"><BR>
<INPUT TYPE="reset" VALUE="Clear Form"
→onClick="return confirm('Are you sure you
→want to clear the form?)">
</FORM></BODY>
</HTML>
```

Figure 4.13 If the user chooses "no" in the confirm box, the text is not erased.

CONFIRMING RESETS

A click on a reset button returns a form to its original state. You can use JavaScript to confirm with the user before submitting or resetting a form. To do this you return **true** or **false** to the event handler, as shown in Script 4.11.

To ask the user to confirm a reset:

> onClick="return confirm('Are you sure you want to clear the form?')"

1. onClick="   "

Within the HTML tag for the reset button, type **onClick=** to trigger a response when the user clicks on the reset button.

OR onReset="   "

Within the HTML tag for the form, type **onReset=** to trigger a response when the user clicks on the reset button.

2.   return

Type **return**. This allows a function or method to return a value to the event handler and stop the form reset.

3.   confirm('Are you sure you want to clear the form?')

Assign any function which returns **true** or **false** to **onClick**. If it returns **false**, JavaScript will stop the form reset.

JavaScript and CGI

CGI provides a means of processing user information on the server. Usually, this information comes from the form elements that the user has filled out.

As mentioned on page 4, JavaScript can replace CGI scripts in some situations, but sometimes you'll still need to send information to the server. You can use JavaScript to improve this process by validating forms before submission.

Forms includes a number of properties (action, method, target, and encoding) which apply specifically to CGI submissions. If you're used to working with CGI, you have probably set these attributes in HTML.

You can also change them in your script with a basic assignment statement. For example, by assigning a new value to action you could divide CGI queries between two servers or use a single HTML form for several CGI applications.

The following two pages discuss some common JavaScript techniques used to complement CGI applications.

Table 4.6

form object	
PROPERTIES	**METHODS**
action URL to which form is submitted	submit() submits form to CGI server
method "get" or "post" method of transfer	**EVENT HANDLERS**
target window name for CGI reply	onSubmit user submits form
encoding MIME type	
elements array of form objects	

Script 4.12 You can use a conditional statement to confirm a form submission.

```
                    script
<HTML><HEAD><TITLE>Form Submission</TITLE>
<SCRIPT LANGUAGE="JavaScript">
<!--HIDE
function checker(theForm) {
   if (confirm("Are you ready to submit
 →this information?")) {
      theForm.submit()
   }
}
//STOP HIDING-->
</SCRIPT></HEAD>
<BODY><FORM ACTION="URL">
<H2>Sign up for our mail-list:<BR><BR>
Name:<INPUT TYPE="text"><BR>
email:<INPUT TYPE="text" onChange=
 →"checker(this.form)"></H2>
</FORM></BODY></HTML>
```

Figure 4.14 The confirm dialog pops up when the user changes the second text field.

TRIGGERING A FORM SUBMISSION

Like a form reset (see page 59) you can make a form submission trigger an event with the button's **onClick** or the form's **onSubmit**.

When the user clicks on the submit button she sends the form data to the URL you assign to **ACTION** in HTML. You can also trigger a form submission from within your script, as in Script 4.12.

To trigger a form submission:

1. function checker(theForm) {

Define a function with one argument (see page 38), a reference to the form.

2. if (confirm("Are you ready to submit this information?")) { theForm.submit() } }

if (

) {   }

Within your function, create an if statement, as discussed on page 67 in the next chapter. The if statement will submit the form only if whatever is between its parentheses () evaluates to **true**.

confirm("Are you ready to submit this information?")

Put **confirm()** within the parentheses of your if statement. You can use **confirm()** because it always returns a Boolean value.

theForm.submit()

Type the argument to address your form. Type **.submit()** to trigger a form submission from your script.

3. onChange = "checker(this.form)"

Use an event handler to trigger your function (see page 32). Pass your function **this.form** to shorten your addressing in the function (see page 33).

VALIDATING A FORM

Almost everyone who spends time on the Web has had the frustrating experience of submitting a form only to get an error message. You have to wait while your form uploads, gets processed, and then finally is sent back to you with an error.

JavaScript can't guarantee that users won't make mistakes, but it can point them out much faster than CGI. By writing a simple form validation function like the one in Script 4.13, you can give the user immediate feedback about what went wrong.

To validate a form:

1. function isBlank(theForm) {

   Define a function with one argument (see page 38), a reference to the form.

2. if (theForm.elements[0].value == "") {

   Type **if** and then the condition you want to check. You will learn about this kind of statement, a conditional, in Chapter 5. For now, you just need to know that the parentheses contain a test, in this case whether the user has filled out an entry.

3. alert("Please enter missing data") }

   If the user hasn't filled out a part of the form, you can alert him to the problem with a dialog like the one in Figure 4.14.

4. else { theForm.submit() } }

   Type **else** followed by a submit command in braces (see page 66 for an explanation of the tabs used in Script 4.13). This statement tells JavaScript to submit the form only if the text field you tested is not empty.

5. onClick="check(this.form)"

   Trigger your validation function with **onClick** in the HTML tag of a button (see page 32). Pass it **this.form** to shorten addressing (see page 33).

Script 4.13 By checking the value of the elements, your script can alert the user to missing responses.

```
<HTML><HEAD><TITLE>Validate Example</TITLE>
<SCRIPT LANGUAGE="JavaScript">
<!--HIDE
function isBlank(theForm) {
    if (theForm.elements[0].value == "" ||
    theForm.elements[1].value == "") {
        alert("Please enter missing data.")
    } else {
        theForm.submit()
    }
}
//STOP HIDING--></SCRIPT></HEAD><BODY><FORM>
<H3>Please enter your first name:
<INPUT TYPE="text" VALUE="" NAME="first"><BR>
your last name:
<INPUT TYPE="text" VALUE="" NAME="last"><BR>
<INPUT TYPE="button" VALUE="submit info"
→onClick="check(this.form)">
</FORM></BODY></HTML>
```

Figure 4.15 A JavaScript form validation function provides immediate feedback on submission problems.

Table 4.7

fileUpload object		my file Browse...
PROPERTIES		**EVENT HANDLERS**
name	value of name attribute	onFocus user focuses on field
value	location of the file	onBlur user leaves field
METHODS		onChange user specifies new
focus()	jump to text field	file
blur()	leave text field	

Script 4.14 The fileUpload element allows the user to choose a file to be sent to the server.

```
script
<HTML><HEAD><TITLE>fileUpload Example</TITLE>
<SCRIPT LANGUAGE="JavaScript">
<!--HIDE
function checkIt() {
    if (document.forms[0].theFile.value == "") {
        alert("Please specify a file to upload.")
        return false
    } else {
        return true
    }
}
//STOP HIDING-->
</SCRIPT></HEAD><BODY>
<H1>Give us your files!!</H1>
<FORM NAME="theForm">
<INPUT TYPE="file" NAME="theFile"><BR>
<INPUT TYPE="submit" VALUE="Upload My File"
→onClick="return checkIt()">
</FORM></BODY></HTML>
```

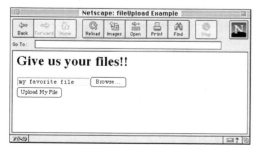

Figure 4.16 You can access and test the path of the file the user specifies.

UPLOADING FILES

Instead of forcing users to bother with FTP, you can use an HTML file upload element to let them choose a file right on your web page. This new element has two parts: a text field and a browse button. The button brings up a dialog box for selecting a file. The text field stores the name of the selected file. When the user submits the form, his file is sent to the server.

For security reasons, JavaScript can read only the name you put in the input tag and the value of the file upload element. You can use **value** to determine if the user has selected a file, as in Script 4.14.

To check if the user has chosen a file to upload:

1. if(document.forms[0].theFile.value == "") {

if(   ) {

Within a checking function (see Script 4.13), type **if** followed by parentheses. This tells JavaScript to continue only if what you put in the parentheses is true.

    document.forms[0].theFile

Address your file upload element (see page 26.)

                    .value

Type a dot and then **value** to access the location of the user's file.

                          == ""

Type the symbol for the equality operator (==) and then a null string (""). This tests if the user has chosen a file.

2. alert("Please specify a file to upload.")

Within the braces of the **if** statement, provide an error message. JavaScript will display it if the user tries to submit the form before choosing a file.

DETERMINING TYPES OF INPUT

At times you may want your function to know what kind of element called it. In this way, a single function can do different things with different elements, as in Script 4.15.

You can get this information by accessing the type property. Every element has a type, which you specify in the input tag. **Type** stores the type of the HTML element, for example **button** or **text**.

To determine which input type called a function:

1. function typer(it) {

Define a function with one argument (see page 38), a reference to the calling form element.

2. alert(it.type) }

> it

Within the function, type the name of the argument.

> .type

Type a dot followed by **type** to address the type property. It stores the text you enter for the type attribute of the input tag.

alert(   ) }

Use this value in your script. Script 4.15 alerts this value.

3. <INPUT TYPE="text" onFocus="typer(this)">

> TYPE="text"

In the body of your HTML document, create an input tag and give it a type. The type property stores this value.

> onFocus="typer(this)"

At the end of the input tag, use an event handler to call your function (see page 32). Pass your function **this** so it can access the caller (see page 33).

Script 4.15 You can use the type property to determine the element which called a function.

```
<HTML>
<HEAD><TITLE>Type Property</TITLE>
<SCRIPT LANGUAGE="JavaScript">
<!--HIDE
function typer(it) {
   alert(it.type)
}
//STOP HIDING-->
</SCRIPT></HEAD>
<BODY><FORM>
<INPUT TYPE="checkbox" onClick="typer(this)">
<INPUT TYPE="text" onFocus= "typer(this)">
<INPUT TYPE="button" VALUE="Press" onClick=
→"typer(this)">
</FORM></BODY>
</HTML>
```

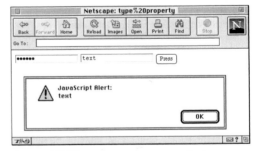

Figure 4.17 The type property stores the input type which you define in HTML.

LOOPS AND CONDITIONALS

5

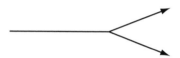

Normal script.

Conditionals allow your script to branch.

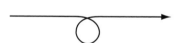

Loops allow your script to repeat a block of statements.

In most of the scripts you have written so far, JavaScript runs each line of code as it reads it. These scripts are said to be linear.

Your scripts will be greatly limited if they can only proceed linearly. Scripts should be able to decide to skip one line of code or read a set of statements more than once. A script that runs linearly can't make these decisions.

In this chapter you will learn the two basic techniques for making a decision in JavaScript. With conditionals, you can test whether code should be run or ignored. Loops, on the other hand, provide an easy way to repeat groups of statements.

WHAT ARE CONDITIONALS?

Conditionals are basic JavaScript decision-makers. JavaScript, like all programming languages, can make only simple decisions. In fact, it can really make only one type of decision.

JavaScript can test a condition which you define. If the test is true, JavaScript will read one set of statements; if the test is false it either reads a second set of statements or continues reading the rest of your script.

You signal most JavaScript conditionals with the keyword if. As in Figure 5.1, you follow this with the condition to be tested and the statements you want the conditional to use. Note that you should tab in your conditional statements as you do with functions.

The condition you specify has to evaluate to a Boolean, **true** or **false**. This Boolean can come from a variable or function. But more often you will compare two values within your conditional statement. You do this by using comparison and logical operators (see pages 66–67).

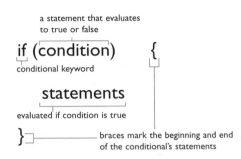

Figure 5.1 When you create a conditional, you tell JavaScript how to make its decision and what to do.

Script 5.1 You can use confirm() as the condition of an if statement.

```
                    script
<HTML>
<HEAD><TITLE>If... Example</TITLE>
<SCRIPT LANGUAGE="JavaScript">
<!--HIDE
function whatIf() {
  if (confirm("Are you over the age of 18?")){
    alert("Go see our smut at www.dirty.old
    →.man.com.")
  }
}
//STOP HIDING-->
</SCRIPT></HEAD>
<BODY onLoad="whatIf()">
</BODY></HTML>
```

Figure 5.2 If the user answers Yes, JavaScript runs the conditional's statements. If he answers No, it ignores them.

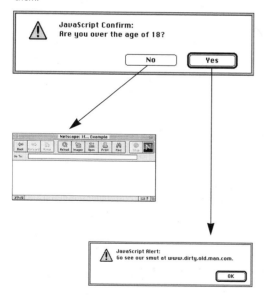

MAKING A SIMPLE DECISION

The if statement is JavaScript's simplest conditional. It tests the condition in parentheses and, if it is true, runs the code in braces. When the conditional is complete the script continues reading the lines that follow it.

To make a simple decision:

> if (confirm("Are you over the age of 18?"))
> { alert("Go see our smut at www.dirty.old
> .man.com.") }

1. if

Type the keyword **if** to signal the beginning of a conditional statement.

2. (   )

Use parentheses after **if** to store the condition you are testing. Remember, this condition must evaluate to a Boolean.

3.   confirm("Are you over the age of 18?")

Put the condition to be tested within the parentheses. Script 5.1 uses a confirm dialog. Because **confirm()** returns the user's response as a Boolean, you can use it as the condition.

4. { alert("Go see our smut at www.dirty.old
.man.com.") }

Within braces, type the statements you want JavaScript to use if the condition is **true**. If the condition is not **true**, JavaScript will ignore these statements and continue reading your script after the close-brace.

COMPARING VALUES

Loops and conditionals use the conditions you give them to determine what to do. Usually, conditions compare two expressions, the left and right *operands*. This comparison results in a Boolean value of **true** or **false**.

To make these comparisons, loops and conditionals require operators other than the assignment operators you learned in Chapter 2. They use what are known as *comparison* and *logical* operators.

Comparison operators determine whether values are equal, and if not, which value is greater. You can use them to compare numbers or strings. When comparing strings, **b** is considered greater than **a**.

To compare values:

```
if (18 <= age.value) {
```

1. if

Type **if** to begin a conditional.

2. ( )

Use parentheses to hold the condition you want to test.

3. 18

Put any legal JavaScript expression after **(**. JavaScript will evaluate this expression, called the left operand, and compare it with the right one.

4. <=

Type one of the comparison operators listed in Table 5.1. Script 5.2 uses **<=** to test whether the left operand is less than or equal to the right operand.

5. age.value

Put the right operand after the comparison operator. Because JavaScript is loosely typed, the two operands can be of different types, as in Script 5.2.

Table 5.1

OPERATOR	COMPARISON
==	returns true if operands are equal
!=	returns true if operands are not equal
>	returns true if left is greater than right
>=	returns true if left is greater than or equal to right
<	returns true if right is greater than left
<=	returns true if right is greater than or equal to left

Script 5.2 Comparison operators determine the relationship between two values.

```
<HTML>
<HEAD><TITLE>Comparison Operator</TITLE>
<SCRIPT LANGUAGE="JavaScript">
<!--HIDE
function analyze(age) {
    if (18 <= age.value) {
        alert("Go see our smut at www.dirty.old.
        →man.com")
    }
}
//STOP HIDING-->
</SCRIPT></HEAD>
<BODY><FORM>
<H2>Enter your age:</H2>
<INPUT TYPE="text" SIZE=4 onChange=
→analyze(this)>
</FORM></BODY></HTML>
```

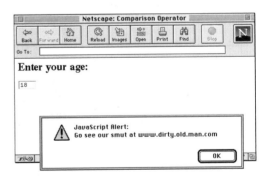

Figure 5.3 You can use a comparison operator to test whether the user claims to be 18 or older.

Table 5.2

OPERATOR	LOGICAL COMPARISON
&&	true if both operands are true ("and")
||	true if either operand is true ("or")
!	true if single operand is false ("not")

Script 5.3 You can use a logical operator to make multiple comparisons.

```
                          script
<HTML>
<HEAD><TITLE>Logical Operator</TITLE>
<SCRIPT LANGUAGE="JavaScript">
<!--HIDE
function analyze(theForm) {
    if (theForm.group[0].checked) &&
    →(theForm.group2[0].checked) {
        alert("Wow, you\'re just the type of cus
        →tomer we\'re looking for.")
    }
}
//STOP HIDING-->
</SCRIPT></HEAD>
<BODY><FORM>
<H2>Are you between the ages of 18 and
24?</H2>
<INPUT TYPE="radio" Name="group"> Yes <BR>
<INPUT TYPE="radio" Name="group"> No <BR>
<H2>Do you like to spend money?</H2>
<INPUT TYPE="radio" Name="group2"> Yes <BR>
<INPUT TYPE="radio" Name="group2"> No <BR>
<INPUT TYPE="button" VALUE="Process Answers"
→onClick="analyze(this.form)">
</FORM></BODY></HTML>
```

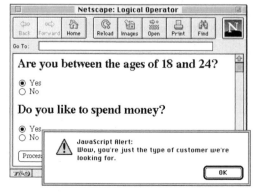

Figure 5.4 A single conditional tests whether the user has checked two radio buttons.

TESTING MULTIPLE CONDITIONS

You can also use a conditional to test more than one value in your script. Script 5.3, for example, only gives an alert if the user has selected two different radio buttons on the page. To include multiple conditions in a single conditional, you use the logical operators, as described in Table 5.2.

To test multiple conditions:

1. function analyze(theForm) {

Define a function with one argument, a reference to the form you are testing.

2. if (theForm.group[0].checked &&
theForm.group2[0]. checked) {

if (
) {

Within your function, write an if statement which you will use to test multiple values.

theForm.group[0].checked

Type the name of the argument and the address of the first property you want to test on the form (see page 26). This property has be **true** or **false**.

&&

Type the desired logical operator. Table 5.2 explains all three. Script 5.3 uses **&&** to check that both buttons are selected.

theForm.group2[0].checked

Follow the logical operator with the name of the argument and the address of the second radio button's checked property. This is the right operand.

3. onClick="analyze(this.form)"

Put an event handler within an HTML tag to call your testing function. Pass it **this.form** to shorten references to the form you are working with. See page 33 for a discussion of the keyword **this**.

USING ALTERNATIVE CODE

If you test a value in your script that doesn't yield **true**, JavaScript will jump to the first line after the conditional's end-brace. You may need your script, however, to read some code in this situation. To accomplish this, you use something called an if-else statement, as in Script 5.4.

The if-else statement adds a second set of statements to your conditional. If your test yields **true**, JavaScript reads the first set of statements, as usual. If it isn't **true**, your script reads this second set.

To use alternative code:

1. function analyze(theForm) {

    Define a function with one argument, a reference to the form you are testing.

2. if (theForm.group[0].checked && theForm.group2[0]. checked) { alert("You're just the type of customer we're looking for.")

    Within your function, create a conditional and give it statements to run (see page 68.)

3. } else { alert("Aww, shucks!") }

    } else

    After the end-brace of the conditional's statements, type a space and the keyword **else**.

        {   }

    Put braces after **else**.

        alert("Aww, shucks!")

    Within these braces, put the statements you want JavaScript to read if your condition is not met.

4. onClick="analyze(this.form)"

    Put an event handler within an HTML tag to call your testing function. Pass it **this.form** to shorten references to the form you are working with (see page 33).

Script 5.4 An if-else statement reads a second set of statements if its condition is not true.

```
<HTML>
<HEAD><TITLE>Logical Operator</TITLE>
<SCRIPT LANGUAGE="JavaScript">
<!--HIDE
function analyze(theForm) {
  if ((theForm.group[0].checked) &&
  →(theForm.group2[0].checked)) {
    alert("You're just the type of cus
  →tomer we're looking for.")
  }
  else {
    alert("Aww, shucks!")
  }
}
//STOP HIDING-->
</SCRIPT></HEAD>
<BODY><FORM>
<H2>Are you between the ages of 18 and
24?</H2>
<INPUT TYPE="radio" Name="group"> Yes <BR>
<INPUT TYPE="radio" Name="group"> No <BR>
<H2>Do you like to spend money?</H2>
<INPUT TYPE="radio" Name="group2"> Yes <BR>
<INPUT TYPE="radio" Name="group2"> No <BR>
<INPUT TYPE="button" VALUE="Process Answers"
→onClick="analyze(this.form)">
</FORM></BODY></HTML>
```

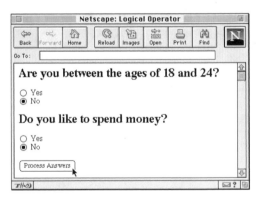

Figure 5.5 If the user doesn't press the correct radio buttons, they are shown a different alert message.

Script 5.5 You can use else-if statements to make your script respond to more than two conditions.

```
<HTML>
<HEAD><TITLE>If else if else</TITLE>
<SCRIPT LANGUAGE="JavaScript">
<!--HIDE
function process() {
  if (document.forms[0].rad[0].checked) {
    location.hash = "#one"
  } else if (document.forms[0].rad[1].checked)
  {
    location.hash = "#two"
  } else {
    location.hash = "#three"
  }
}
//STOP HIDING-->
</SCRIPT></HEAD>
<BODY><FORM>
<H3> Number of books you want to order:</H3>
<INPUT TYPE="radio" NAME="rad" CHECKED>
1-5<BR>
<INPUT TYPE="radio" NAME="rad">6-49<BR>
<INPUT TYPE="radio" NAME="rad">
50 and up<BR></FORM>
<A HREF="#" onClick="process()">
Order Information</A>
</BODY></HTML>
```

Figure 5.6 You can tell JavaScript to do different things for each of three options.

USING MULTIPLE ALTERNATIVES

You can now tell JavaScript to do two things after it makes a decision: read a set of statements when the test yields true, and read another set when it doesn't. By introducing another condition, you can give your conditional a third set of statements.

You can introduce any number of options to your conditional by adding else-if statements. Script 5.5 tells JavaScript "If the first option is checked, read these statements. If the second option is checked, read different statements. In any other case, read a third set of statements." You create the second sentence by using an else-if statement.

To use multiple alternatives:

1. if (document.forms[0].rad[0].checked) {
   location.hash = "#one"

   Create a conditional test and follow it with the desired statements.

2. } else if (document.forms[0].rad[1].checked)
   { location.hash = "#two"

   } else if

   After the end-brace of your first condition, type **else if**. This tells JavaScript that you are introducing a second condition.

   (document.forms[0].rad[1].checked)

   Put your second condition with parentheses after **else if**. Script 5.5 tests whether the user has checked the second radio button.

   { location.hash = "#two"

   Follow your second condition with { and a second set of statements which the script will read if this condition is met.

3. } else { location.hash = "#three" }

   If you want, you can follow your second condition with a default set of statements (see page 70).

USING SHORTHAND CONDITIONALS

JavaScript allows you to create a conditional with just a few keystrokes. *Conditional expressions* are shorthand versions of if-else statements. Besides having a shorter syntax, conditional expressions always return a value.

Conditional expressions don't look like the other syntax you've seen in JavaScript, but if you master them you'll find them quite useful. Script 5.6, for example, assigns only a short line of code to an image source to decide which image to display to the user.

To use shorthand conditionals:

```
<IMG SRC="&{(confirm('Would you prefer
Clinton to Dole?')) ? 'clinton.gif' : 'dole.gif'};">
```

1. **<IMG SRC=   >**

    Within an HTML tag, type the name of the attribute want to assign your conditional expression to. Script 5.6 assigns it to an image source.

    OR myVar =

    You can also assign the conditional expression to a variable in your script.

2. **"&{   };"**

    Use the characters discussed on page 43 to create a JavaScript entity. Script 5.7 uses quotation marks because HTML requires them for image sources.

3. **(confirm("Would you prefer Clinton to Dole?"))**

    Type your condition within parentheses.

4. **?**

    Follow it with **?** to signal that you are using a conditional expression.

5. **'clinton.gif' : 'dole.gif'**

    Type the values for the conditional, separated by a colon. This example returns **'clinton.gif'** if the condition is true and **'dole.gif'** if the condition is false.

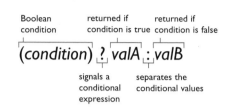

(condition) ? valA : valB

Boolean condition | returned if condition is true | returned if condition is false
signals a conditional expression | separates the conditional values

Figure 5.7 A conditional expression

Script 5.6 You can use conditional expressions in place of an if-else statement which returns a value.

```
<HTML>
<HEAD>
<TITLE>Conditional Expression</TITLE>
</HEAD>
<BODY>
<IMG SRC="&{(confirm('Would you prefer Clinton
→to Dole?')) ? 'clinton.gif' : 'dole.gif'};">
</BODY>
</HTML>
```

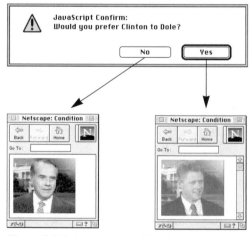

Figure 5.8 By inserting a conditional expression in a JavaScript entity you can let the user choose the content of a page.

USING SHORTHAND CONDITIONALS

REPEATING CODE WITH A LOOP

If you needed to check the value of every element in a large form, you could address each individually, but your script wouldn't be very efficient. You'd do much better to use what's called a *loop*. A loop repeats a set of JavaScript statements until its condition is false.

Script 5.7 uses a while loop. The while loop uses the same syntax as the conditional and is the simplest kind of loop. JavaScript runs its statements repeatedly until its condition is false.

To repeat code with a loop:

while (ans != num) { ans=prompt(Guess a number between 0 and 10:") }

1. while

Type **while** anywhere in your script to signal the beginning of your while loop.

2.   (ans != num)

Type your while loop's condition within parentheses. Script 5.7 compares a variable storing the user's guess with one storing the correct number.

3.   {
                                      }

As in a conditional, follow your condition with braces.

4.   ans=prompt(Guess a number between 0 and 10:")

Put the statements you want your loop to repeat within the braces. Script 5.7 prompts the user to enter another guess.

Script 5.7 You can use the while loop to repeat a group of statements.

```
script
<HTML>
<HEAD><TITLE>While Example</TITLE>
<SCRIPT LANGUAGE="JavaScript">
<!--HIDE
function guessIt() {
  var num = Math.round(Math.random() * 10)
  var ans = 0
  while (ans != num) {
    ans = prompt("Guess a number between 0
     →and 10:")
  }
  alert("Congratulations!!!!")
}
//STOP HIDING-->
</SCRIPT></HEAD>
<BODY onLoad="guessIt()">
</BODY></HTML>
```

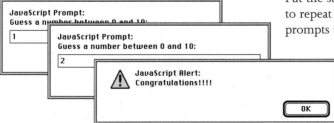

Figure 5.9 JavaScript prompts the user until she guesses the correct number.

COUNTING WITH A FOR LOOP

The while loop runs a set of statements any number of times. To work with different information each time your loops repeats, however, you need a for loop.

The for loop uses a *counter* to change a value each time it repeats. When you define your for loop, you specify information about the counter in addition to your loop's condition.

To count with a for loop:

```
for (var i = 1; i <= 10; i++) {
document.write("<H1>" + i + "</H1>")
alert("Wow, we're counting!") }
```

1. for (   )

Type **for** anywhere in your script and follow it with parentheses to mark the beginning of a for loop.

2.   var i = 1

Use the equals sign to assign a starting value for your counter. Traditionally, for loops use the variable i. You can declare the variable (see page 17) here if you haven't done so already.

3.   ; i <= 10

Put your loop's condition after a semi-colon. The loop will stop when this condition is no longer true. Usually you will use the comparison operators to compare your counter with a fixed value.

4.   i++

After a semicolon, type your loop's counting expression. You can use the incrementing operators listed on page 22. Script 5.8, for example, uses **++** to add one to the counter with each repetition.

5.   {
document.write("<H1>" + i + "</H1>")
alert("Wow, we're counting!") }

After), type your statements inside of braces. You will probably want to use your counter variable in these statements.

Script 5.8 When defining a for loop, you give information about a counter variable.

```
<HTML>
<HEAD><TITLE>The For Loop</TITLE>
<SCRIPT LANGUAGE="JavaScript">
<!--HIDE
function count() {
   for (var i = 1; i <= 10; i++) {
      document.write("<H1>" + i + "</H1>")
      alert("Wow, we're counting!")
   }
}
//STOP HIDING-->
</SCRIPT></HEAD>
<BODY onLoad="count()"><FORM>
</FORM></BODY>
</HTML>
```

Figure 5.10 JavaScript can count using a for loop. The alert in this example simply slows down the process.

Script 5.9 You can use the for in loop to cycle through the properties of an object.

```
script

<HTML>
<HEAD><TITLE>For in Example</TITLE>
<SCRIPT LANGUAGE="JavaScript">
<!--HIDE
function listIt() {
   var info = ""
   for(prop in document) {
      alert(prop + " is " + document[prop])
   }
}
//STOP HIDING-->
</SCRIPT>
<BODY><FORM NAME="theForm">
<INPUT TYPE="button" VALUE="Document Info"
→onClick="listIt()">
</FORM></BODY></HTML>
```

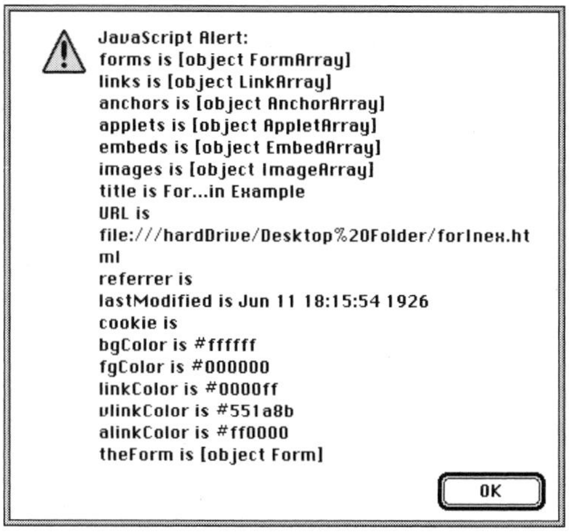

```
JavaScript Alert:
forms is [object FormArray]
links is [object LinkArray]
anchors is [object AnchorArray]
applets is [object AppletArray]
embeds is [object EmbedArray]
images is [object ImageArray]
title is For...in Example
URL is
file:///hardDrive/Desktop%20Folder/forInex.ht
ml
referrer is
lastModified is Jun 11 18:15:54 1926
cookie is
bgColor is #ffffff
fgColor is #000000
linkColor is #0000ff
vlinkColor is #551a8b
alinkColor is #ff0000
theForm is [object Form]

                                    OK
```

Figure 5.11 This dialog lists all of the properties of document.

WORKING WITH PROPERTIES

JavaScript includes a third kind of loop specifically designed so that you can work with all of an object's properties. This is called the for in loop. You would normally use this loop with objects that you make (see page 34), but you can also use it to learn about the JavaScript hierarchy. Figure 5.11, for example, displays all of the properties of **document**.

To use the for in loop you only have to specify the object you want to work with.

To work with every property of an object:

1. for (prop in document) {

for (   ) {

Type **for** followed by parentheses anywhere in your script to begin a JavaScript loop.

   prop

Type the name of your counter variable. You do not have to declare this variable anywhere. With each repetition, JavaScript will automatically fill it with the text value of the next property.

   in

Type **in** to tell JavaScript that this is a for in loop.

   document

Address the object whose properties you want to look at. Script 5.9 looks at the properties of the document object.

2. alert(prop + " is " + document[prop]) }

Type the desired statements within braces. You can refer to the current property by typing the object address followed by the counter in braces.

AVOIDING INFINITE LOOPS

If your loop's condition is never false, JavaScript will never break from its statements and the user's browser will freeze in what is called an infinite loop. To avoid this common programming mistake, you should always check that your condition will be met at some point.

Common loop errors:

1. **Comparing a variable with itself.** The loop in Script 5.10 will never stop, because **i + 2** is always two greater than i. Anytime you compare a variable with itself you risk an infinite loop.

2. **Testing equivalence.** You'll generally want to stop your loop when the counter reaches some fixed value. You can test for equivalence by using **==** in your loop's condition, but then you have to worry that the loop will skip over your breaking condition. Instead, try and use **<=** if adding to your counter and **>=** if you are subtracting from it.

3. **Floating-point comparisons.** Don't forget that JavaScript's tends to do unpredictable things with floating-point numbers. Try to work only with integers in your comparisons.

Script 5.10 This seemingly harmless script will actually force the user to quit her browser.

```
script
<HTML>
<HEAD><TITLE>Infinite Jest</TITLE>
<SCRIPT LANGUAGE="JavaScript">
<!--HIDE
function doCount() {
  var i = eval(document.theForm.input.value)
  while( i < (i + 2)) {
    i += 1
    alert(i)
  }
}
//STOP HIDING-->
</SCRIPT></HEAD>
<BODY><H2><FORM NAME="theForm">
Enter starting number to begin counting:
<INPUT TYPE="text" NAME="input" onBlur=
→"doCount()"><BR>
</FORM></BODY></HTML>
```

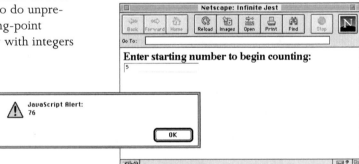

Figure 5.12 This script compares the counter to itself and begins a never-ending series of alerts.

AVOIDING INFINITE LOOPS

Script 5.11 You can use a nested conditional to cycle through each of a form's elements.

```
                    script
<HTML>
<HEAD>
<TITLE>Nesting Example</TITLE>
<SCRIPT LANGUAGE="JavaScript">
<!--HIDE
function search(aForm) {
  for (var i=0;i < aForm.rad.length;i++){
    if (aForm.rad[i].checked) {
      alert("Radio " + (i+1) + " is select
      ↪ed.")
    }
  }
}
//STOP HIDING-->
</SCRIPT></HEAD>
<BODY><FORM>
<INPUT TYPE="radio" NAME="rad" CHECKED>
Choice 1<BR>
<INPUT TYPE="radio" NAME="rad">
Choice 2<BR>
<INPUT TYPE="radio" NAME="rad">
Choice 3<BR>
<INPUT TYPE="button" VALUE="Analyze"
↪onClick="search(this.form)">
</FORM></BODY>
</HTML>
```

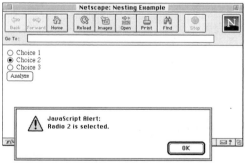

Figure 5.13 This script can check as many radio buttons as you define in your HTML.

TESTING SEVERAL FORM ELEMENTS

By placing conditionals within loops, you can test a condition for many different parts of your page. This process is called *nesting*. You nest things in JavaScript any time you place them inside one another. When nesting conditionals in loops you should pay extra attention to include all of the parentheses and braces.

To test several form elements:

1. for (var i=0; i < aForm.rad.length; i++) {

for (   ) {

Type **for** and parentheses to begin your for loop.

var i=0;

Define a counter variable with an initial value of zero. Type ; after this assignment.

i < aForm.rad.length;

Define a condition that will stop the loop when it has checked all the entries in the array. The loop in Script 5.11 repeats for each radio button with the same name.

i++

Type **i++** to increase your counter by one with each repetition.

2. if (aForm.rad[i].checked) {

Press tab and type a conditional as the first statement of the loop. Script 5.11 checks each radio button to see if it has been checked.

3. alert("Radio " + (i+1) + " is selected.")

Put your conditional's statements within braces. Be sure to follow the statements with two end braces: one for the conditional and one for the loop.

STOPPING A LOOP

As you saw on the previous page, you can use a nested conditional to determine which form elements the user has checked. If you're checking radio buttons, for example, there is no reason to continue once you've found the one that the user has selected. In this type of situation, you can use the break statement to stop the loop before it reaches its end, as in Script 5.12.

After a loop finishes, its counter stores the value you specified as the loop's condition. By using **break** as the single statement of a conditional, you can find the element you are looking for and access it in the rest of your script through the counter.

To stop a loop:

1. for (var i=0; i < aForm.rad.length; i++) {
        if (aForm.rad[i].checked == true) {

Create a nested conditional to search for a selected form element, as described on the previous page.

2. break }

Type **break** as the single statement of your nested conditional. This stops the loop when i is the index number of the selected element.

3. alert("Radio"+ (i+1) + "is selected.")

You can use the counter variable elsewhere in your function or script. If you used this variable without **break**, it would store **3**, the first value that makes the condition false, and display as four. Because you used break, it stores the number of the selected button, in this case 1, and displays as two.

Script 5.12 You should use the break statement in a conditional if you want to work with the counter value elsewhere in your script.

```
script
<HTML>
<HEAD><TITLE>The Break Statement</TITLE>
<SCRIPT LANGUAGE="JavaScript">
<!--HIDE
function search(theForm) {
   for (var i=0;i<theForm.radArray.length;i++){
      if (theForm.radArray[i].checked == true) {
         break
      }
   }
   alert("Radio " + (i+1) + " is selected.")
}
//STOP HIDING-->
</SCRIPT></HEAD>
<BODY><FORM>
<INPUT TYPE="radio" NAME="radArray" CHECKED>
Choice 1<BR>
<INPUT TYPE="radio" NAME="radArray">
Choice 2<BR>
<INPUT TYPE="radio" NAME="radArray">
Choice 3<BR>
<INPUT TYPE="button" VALUE="Analyze" onClick=
→"search(this.form)">
</FORM></BODY>
</HTML>
```

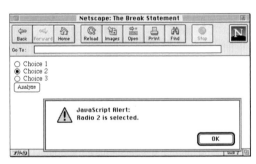

Figure 5.14 You can use break to work with the counter elsewhere in your script.

Figure 5.15 If you don't use break, you'll get a meaningless alert.

Script 5.13 A continue statement sends the script back to the top of the loop.

```
                    script
<HTML>
<HEAD>
<TITLE>The For Loop</TITLE>
<SCRIPT LANGUAGE="JavaScript">
<!--HIDE
function count() {
   for (var i = 1; i <= 10; i++) {
      if (i == 6) {
         continue
      }
      document.write("<H1>" + i + "</H1>")
   }
}
//STOP HIDING-->
</SCRIPT>
</HEAD>
<BODY onLoad="count()">
</BODY>
</HTML>
```

Figure 5.16 When the counter equals 6, JavaScript skips the document.write().

Making Exceptions in a Loop

Although **continue** sounds like it might do just the opposite of **break**, JavaScript couldn't do much with a keyword that let a loop keep going unchanged. Rather, the continue statement sends JavaScript back to the top of the loop.

You can use **continue** to make an exception in your loop. Script 5.13, for example, tells JavaScript to skip the rest of the loop's statements if i equals six.

To make exceptions in a loop:

1. for (var i=1; i<=10; i++) {

Create a for loop (see page 74). This loop will read its statements each time the counter is incremented.

2. if (i == 6) { continue }

if

As the first statement of this for loop, type **if** to begin a nested conditional.

(i == 6)

Within parentheses, compare the loop's counter with the specific value that you want to avoid.

{ continue }

Type **continue** as the single statement of the conditional. When i=6, JavaScript will jump back to the top of the for loop instead of reading its other statements.

SHORTENING ADDRESSES

JavaScript's hierarchy is clear and exact, but it can be annoying to always have to type long addresses. JavaScript includes **this** to shorten addresses (see page 33) and includes the with statement for the same purpose.

A with statement allows you to abbreviate addresses that share the same beginning.

To shorten an address:

1. with (document.forms[0]) {

with

Type **with** to signal the beginning of a with statement.

(document.forms[0])

Within parentheses specify a JavaScript address (see page 26). Script 5.14 refers to the elements of a form.

2. alert(elements[i].type) }

Put your statements within the braces. To refer to an element, as in Script 5.14, just type **elements[ ]** and its index number within the brackets.

Script 5.14 You can use with to save keystrokes.

```
<HTML><HEAD>
<TITLE>With Example</TITLE>
<SCRIPT LANGUAGE="JavaScript">
<!--HIDE
function checker() {
    with (document.forms[0]) {
        for (i=0;i<length;i++) {
        alert(elements[i].type)
        alert(name)
        }
    }
}
//STOP HIDING-->
</SCRIPT></HEAD>
<BODY onLoad="checker()">
<FORM>
<INPUT TYPE="text" VALUE="Enter your
text"><BR><BR>
Advanced
<INPUT TYPE="checkbox"><BR><BR>
<SELECT>
<OPTION>item1
<OPTION>item2
</SELECT></FORM></BODY>
</HTML>
```

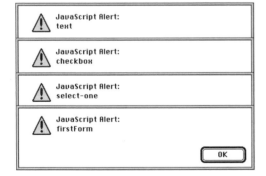

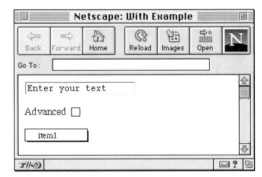

Figure 5.17 This script uses with to shorten the addresses used to trigger these alerts.

STRINGS AND NUMBERS

As you saw in Chapter 1, JavaScript allows you to work with three types of information: strings, numbers, and Booleans. If the user types a number in a text box, JavaScript stores it as a string, but to work with it as a number, you'll need to convert it. You will often need to convert between JavaScript's three types. You should keep in mind the following general rules when converting between different types:

Everything is a string. A string can store all kinds of characters, so it can easily contain numbers or the words "true" and "false". Because of this, JavaScript has no problem pretending that Booleans and numbers are strings. In fact, it does it automatically when your script requires.

Making numbers. There is no way to represent letters or words as numbers. Because of this, JavaScript won't make this change for you. Instead, you need to convert your string into a number. This chapter gives you three different ways to do this.

CONVERTING STRINGS TO NUMBERS

If a user enters a number into a text field, JavaScript reads the value of that field as a string. To work with this value numerically, you need to convert its type. JavaScript includes three built-in functions that you can use to convert strings into numbers.

You will most often use **eval()** to convert text entered by the user into a number. **Eval()** reads the text you give it as though it were a part of the script—its conversion is just a side effect. For some purposes, such as testing lines of code (see Script 6.1), you may want to use the eval command for its original purpose.

To convert strings to numbers:

document.forms[0].out.value = eval(document.forms[0].field.value)

1. document.forms[0].field.value

Within your script, address the text in a text field (see page 26).

2.   eval( )

Type **eval** and surround your string with parentheses. This converts whatever is inside into a piece of JavaScript code. If you give **eval()** a string containing numbers, it turns this into a real numerical value.

3. document.forms[0].out.value =

Once you have converted it, you can use the equals sign to assign the new number to a variable for later use.

Script 6.1 You can use eval() to let the user enter numbers for your script.

```
<HTML>
<HEAD><TITLE>Eval()</TITLE>
<SCRIPT LANGUAGE="JavaScript">
<!--HIDE
function evaluate() {
    document.forms[0].out.value =
    →eval(document.forms[0].field.value)
}
//STOP HIDING-->
</SCRIPT></HEAD>
<BODY><FORM>
<TEXTAREA ROWS="8" COLS="30" NAME="field"
onBlur="evaluate()">Enter JavaScript
</TEXTAREA>
<TEXTAREA ROWS="8" COLS="30" NAME="out">
</TEXTAREA>
</FORM></BODY>
</HTML>
```

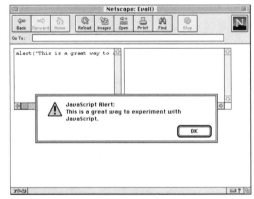

Figure 6.1 The left text block accepts an entry and the right side tries to evaluate it as JavaScript code. A built-in version of this is available in Navigator by typing "javascript:" in the location field.

Script 6.2 You can use parseInt() and parseFloat() to convert text entered by the user to a particular type of number.

```
<HTML>
<HEAD><TITLE>Parsing Example</TITLE>
<SCRIPT LANGUAGE="JavaScript">
<!--HIDE
function parseIt() {
    var a = parseInt(document.it.num.value)
    var b = parseFloat(document.it.num.value)
    theForm.out1.value = a + 2
    theForm.out2.value = b + 2
}
//STOP HIDING-->
</SCRIPT></HEAD>
<BODY><FORM NAME="it">
<INPUT TYPE="text" NAME="num"> + 2 = <BR>
using parseInt():
<INPUT TYPE="text" NAME="out1"><BR>
using parseFloat():
<INPUT TYPE="text" NAME="out2"><BR><BR>
<INPUT TYPE="button" VALUE="parse" onClick=
→"parseIt(this.form)">
</FORM></BODY></HTML>
```

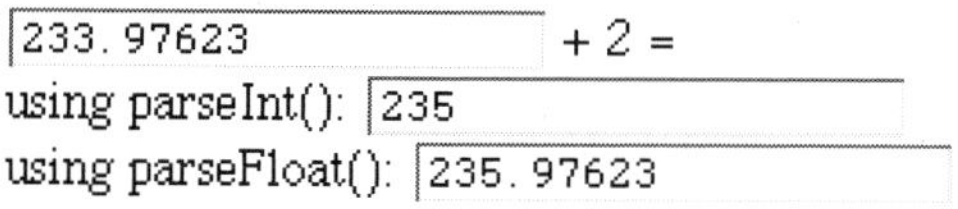

233.97623	+ 2 =
using parseInt():	235
using parseFloat():	235.97623

Figure 6.2 You can use the parsing functions to convert strings to different types of numbers.

CONVERTING STRINGS TO INTEGERS

As you saw on page 21, JavaScript can work with two kinds of numbers: integer and floating-point. If you want JavaScript to treat text entered by the user as a specific kind of number, use **parseInt()** to convert to an integer or **parseFloat()** to convert to a floating-point, or decimal.

You'll also want to use these commands in situations where you can't be sure that the user will enter a number. If you give a letter to **eval()**, you'll get an error message, whereas **parseInt()** and **parseFloat()** will return NaN, which stands for "not a number".

To convert strings to integers:

var a = parseInt(document.it.num.value)

1.   parseInt(   )

Within your script, type **parseInt** followed by parentheses to tell JavaScript that you want to convert to an integer.

OR   parseFloat(   )

Type **parseFloat** followed by parentheses to convert to a floating-point (decimal) number.

2.   document.it.num.value

Type a number surrounded by quotation marks or the address of a text field (see page 26). If this number includes decimal places, **parseInt()** will throw them out, as in Figure 6.2.

3. var a =

Create a variable and assign the new integer to it with the equals sign. You can now access the converted number through this variable.

CONVERTING NUMBERS TO STRINGS

You can almost always let JavaScript take care of converting numbers to strings as necessary. However, you may need to do this explicitly so that you can display the number in a particular base (see page 21). This is particularly helpful if you need to work with HTML hexadecimal color codes.

To convert numbers to strings:

document.forms[0].outfield.value = num.toString(base)

1. num

Type the name of a variable which stores a number. Script 6.3 creates one to hold a number chosen by the user.

2.   .toString(   )

Type a dot followed by **toString** to tell JavaScript that you want to make your number into a string.

3.   base

If you want to display the number in a base other than 10 (see page 21), insert a number between 2 and 16 in the parentheses.

4. document.forms[0].outfield.value =

Address the text of a text box (see page 26) and use the equals sign to assign it the string you made. This displays the converted number in the field.

Script 6.3 ToString() converts numbers to strings.

```
                    script
<HTML>
<HEAD><TITLE>toString() Example</TITLE>
<SCRIPT LANGUAGE="JavaScript">
<!--HIDE
function convert(numStr, baseStr) {
    num = eval(numStr)
    base = eval(baseStr)
    document.forms[0].outfield.value =
    →num.toString(base)
}
//STOP HIDING-->
</SCRIPT></HEAD>
<BODY><FORM>
Enter a number: <INPUT TYPE="text" NAME="num">
<BR>and a base to convert it to:
<INPUT TYPE="text" SIZE=2 onBlur="convert
→(this.form.num.value, this.value)"><BR><BR>
<INPUT TYPE="text" NAME="outfield" SIZE=60>
</FORM></BODY></HTML>
```

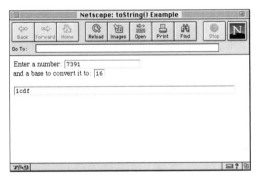

Figure 6.3 You use toString() to convert numbers to a particular base for display.

Script 6.4 Typeof tells you the data type of an expression as a string value.

```
                   script
<HTML><HEAD><TITLE>Parsing Example</TITLE>
<SCRIPT LANGUAGE="JavaScript">
<!--HIDE
var disp
function myFunction() {
}
function showMe() {
  disp = "4 is of type " + (typeof 4) + ".\n"
  disp += "4.57746 is of type " + (typeof
  →4.57746) + ".\n"
  disp += "foo is of type " + (typeof "foo") +
  →".\n"
  disp += "true is of type " + (typeof true) +
  →".\n"
  disp += myFunction + "is of type " + (typeof
  →myFunction) + ".\n"
  disp += document.forms + " is of type " +
  →(typeof document.forms) + ".\n"
  disp += "null is of type " + (typeof null) +
  →".\n"
  alert(disp)
}
//STOP HIDING--></SCRIPT></HEAD>
<BODY><FORM>
<INPUT TYPE="button" VALUE="show me"
→onClick="showMe()">
</FORM></BODY></HTML>
```

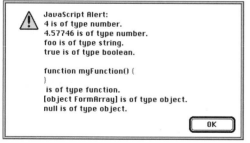

Figure 6.4 You can use typeof as a debugging tool. Put it within an alert to display the type of a variable.

DETERMINING A VARIABLE TYPE

If you aren't sure what type of value a variable holds you can test it with **typeof**. This can be a useful tool for debugging your scripts. **Typeof** gives you the name of the type, as in Figure 6.5.

To determine the type of a variable:

disp = "4 is of type" + (typeof 4)

1.   **typeof**

   Within your script or function, type **typeof** to tell JavaScript that you want to know the type of the variable that follows it.

2.   4

   After a space, enter the name of the variable you wish to test. **Typeof** will give you its type as one of the following strings: **string**, **number**, **boolean**, **undefined**, **function**, or **object**.

3. disp = "4 is of type" + (   )

   You can then use this value in your script. Script 6.4 concatenates a number of these values to a variable (see page 23) which it then displays.

DETERMINING INDIVIDUAL LETTERS

As you saw on page 19, JavaScript calls series of characters strings. JavaScript considers every variable that stores text an instance (see page 34) of the String object.

JavaScript lets you manipulate and test string variables with the methods listed in Table 6.1.

To determine individual letters of text:

1. var userText = document.forms[0].field.value

Within your script, declare a variable and assign a string to it (see page 19). This creates an instance of the String object.

2. alert(userText.charAt(4) + " is the fifth character in your entry.")

    userText.charAt( )

In the same function, type the name of your new variable followed by .charAt().

    4

Put in the parentheses the index number of the character you want to test. JavaScript counts the first character as **0**.

alert(+ "is the fifth character in your entry.")

You can then use this value in your script. Script 6.5 displays the fifth character of whatever the user types into a text field.

Table 6.1

String object	
METHODS (NON-HTML)	
charAt(n)	returns character before n
indexOf(text)	returns first occurrence of text in string
lastIndexOf(text)	returns last occurrence of text in string
split(text)	returns array of substrings all split at text
substring(n,m)	returns substring from character n to one before character m
toLowerCase()	returns string in lowercase
toUpperCase()	returns string in uppercase

Script 6.5 The charAt method returns a single character from the string. JavaScript numbers the first character as zero.

```
<HTML>
<HEAD>
<TITLE>String.charAt() Example</TITLE>
<SCRIPT LANGUAGE="JavaScript">
<!--HIDE
function stringer() {
    var userText = document.forms[0].field
    →.value
    alert(userText.charAt(4) + " is the fifth
    →character in your entry.")
}
//STOP HIDING-->
</SCRIPT></HEAD>
<BODY><FORM>
<INPUT TYPE="text" NAME="field" VALUE="string"
→onChange="stringer()">
</FORM></BODY></HTML>
```

Table 6.2

String object

METHODS (HTML)

anchor()	surrounds string with anchor tag
big()	surrounds string with BIG tag
blink()	surrounds string with BLINK tag
bold()	surrounds string with B tag
fixed()	surrounds string with TT tag
fontcolor(n)	given color, surrounds string with FONT COLOR tags
fontsize(n)	given size, surrounds string with FONT SIZE tags
italics()	surrounds string with italics tag
link(URL)	given a URL, surrounds string with link tag
small()	surrounds string with SMALL tag
strike()	surrounds string with STRIKE tag
sub()	surrounds string with SUB tag
sup()	surrounds string with SUP tag

Script 6.6 You can use methods of the String object to format text entered by the user.

```
<HTML>
<TITLE>HTML String Methods</TITLE>
<BODY>
<SCRIPT LANGUAGE="JavaScript">
<!--HIDE
var str = prompt("what do you say there,
→sonny?")
document.write(str.blink().fontsize(7))
//STOP HIDING-->
</SCRIPT>
</BODY></HTML>
```

FORMATTING TEXT FOR DISPLAY

You'll often want to put HTML tags around a string to display it on the page (see page 11). You could add the tags manually by concatenating them (see page 23), but this isn't very efficient. Instead, you should use the HTML methods for strings. These do the exact same thing, but save you a few keystrokes.

To format text for display:

1. var str = prompt("what do you say there, sonny?")

Create a string variable which stores the desired text (see page 19).

2. document.write(str.blink().fontsize(7))

        str

Type the name of your string variable.

        .blink()

Type a dot and the name of the formatting you want to apply followed by parentheses. This surrounds your text with the appropriate tag.

        .fontsize(7)

To use multiple types of formatting, you can simply add the appropriate method with a dot before it, as in Script 6.6.

document.write( )

To display the formatted text, put it within the parentheses of document.write().

Figure 6.5 Here, JavaScript asks the user to enter some text, and then formats it for display.

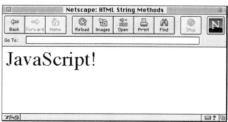

VALIDATING A NUMERICAL ENTRY

Everybody makes mistakes sometimes, and web users are no exception. If you need to be sure that the user has entered a number, you can check it with JavaScript before the form is submitted, as in Script 6.9.

To validate a numerical entry:

1. function validate(data) {

Create a function with one argument (see page 38), the text to check.

2. for (var i=0; i < data.length; i++) {

Within this function, create a for loop (see page 74) that cycles through each character until the end of the text.

3. var digit = data.charAt(i)

Use **charAt()** (see page 87) with your counter variable in parentheses, and assign this character to a new variable.

4. if (digit < "0" || digit > "9") {

if (   ) {

Within the loop place an if statement (see page 67).

    digit < "0"

Check if the character in the current position is less than zero. This lets you screen out symbols and punctuation.

       digit > "9"

Check if the current character is greater than nine. This eliminates letters.

       ||

Link your two conditions with an "or" (see page 69).

5. alert(digit + " is not a number.")

Use a display function to alert the user to the error she has made (see page 14).

Script 6.9 A form validation function can check that data is valid before submitting it.

```
<HTML>
<HEAD><TITLE>Form Validation</TITLE>
<SCRIPT LANGUAGE="JavaScript">
<!--HIDE
function validate(data) {
  for (var i=0; i < data.length; i++) {
    var digit = data.charAt(i)
    if (digit < "0" || digit > "9") {
      if (digit == ",") {
        alert("Leave out commas.")
        return false
      } else {
        alert(digit + " is not a number.")
        return false
      }
    }
  }
  document.forms[0].submit("#")
  return true
}
//STOP HIDING-->
</SCRIPT></HEAD>
<BODY><FORM>
<H2>Guess the number of miles between Paris
→and New York:</H2>
<INPUT TYPE="text">
<INPUT TYPE="submit" VALUE="submit" onClick=
→"return validate(this.form.elements
→[0].value)">
</FORM></BODY>
</HTML>
```

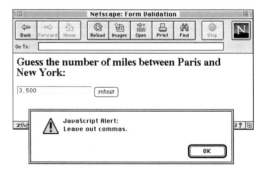

Figure 6.8 This script halts the submit process and tells the user her text was incorrectly entered.

Script 6.10 To change the range of the random method, multiply by the range and add the minimum value.

```
<HTML>
<HEAD><TITLE>The Math Object</TITLE>
<SCRIPT LANGUAGE="JavaScript">
<!--HIDE
function doMath(x) {
   var min = eval(x.elements[0].value)
   var max = eval(x.elements[1].value)
   var ran = Math.random() * (max - min) + min
   alert(ran)
}
//STOP HIDING-->
</SCRIPT></HEAD>
<BODY><FORM>
<H2>Enter min and max for random number:</H2>
<INPUT TYPE="text" VALUE="min" SIZE=3>
<INPUT TYPE="text" VALUE="max" SIZE=3
→onChange="doMath(this.form)">
</FORM></BODY>
</HTML>
```

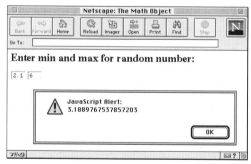

Figure 6.9 You can convert JavaScript's random numbers to any range.

GENERATING A RANDOM NUMBER

JavaScript makes it easy to perform math operations and access common mathmatical constants. You'll need these tools if you want your page to work with numbers.

To make a page different each time the user visits, you use **random()** to generate a random number. You can find the technique to randomize an image on page 96. If you want to be sure that everyone can use your page, you'll want to avoid **random()**, which is new to Navigator 3.0 for Mac and Windows platforms. We provide an alternate technique on page 130.

To generate a random number:

var ran=Math.random() * (max - min) + min

1.   Math.random()

   Type **Math** to address the Math object, then **.random** and parentheses to generate a random number between zero and one.

2.   * (max - min)

   Multiply the result by the difference between the highest and lowest desired values. This increases the range of numbers that you might get.

3.   + min

   Add the lowest desired value.

4. var ran=

   Create a variable and use the equals sign to store your new random number in it for later use (see page 21).

USING A MATHEMATICAL CONSTANT

To make calculations easier, JavaScript stores several common mathematical constants as properties of the Math object. To differentiate them from other properties, you type these constants in all capital letters.

To use a mathematical constant:

```
document.write("<H2> + Math.SQRT2 +
" * " + Math.SQRT2 + " = 2")
```

1.   Math

Type **Math** to tell JavaScript that you are using one of its properties.

2.   .SQRT2

Type a dot followed by the name of the constant you wish to access in all upper-case. You can use this address as a stand-in for the complete number.

3. document.write("<H2> +   +
" * " +   + " = 2")

Use this math constant in your script. Script 6.11 displays an equation to the user (see page 11).

Table 6.3

Math object

PROPERTIES

E	base of natural logarithms (2.718...)
LN2	natural logarithm of 2 (0.693...)
LN10	natural logarithm of 10 (2.302...)
LOG2E	base two logarithm of e (1.442...)
LOG10E	base ten logarithm of e (0.434...)
PI	ratio of circumference to diameter (3.14159...)
SQRT1_2	square root of one-half (0.707...)
SQRT2	square root of two (1.414...)

Script 6.11 The Math object stores common mathematical constants.

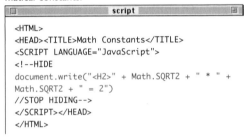

```
<HTML>
<HEAD><TITLE>Math Constants</TITLE>
<SCRIPT LANGUAGE="JavaScript">
<!--HIDE
document.write("<H2>" + Math.SQRT2 + " * " +
Math.SQRT2 + " = 2")
//STOP HIDING-->
</SCRIPT></HEAD>
</HTML>
```

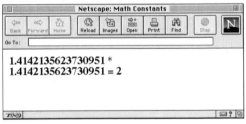

Figure 6.10 You can use the properties of Math to perform common calculations.

USING A MATHEMATICAL CONSTANT

Table 6.4

Math object

METHODS

abs(n)	returns absolute value of n
acos(n)	returns arc cosine of n
asin(n)	returns arc sine of n
atan(n)	returns arc tangent of n
atan2(n,m)	returns angle of polar coordinate
ceil(n)	rounds up to next integer
cos(n)	returns cosine of n
exp(n)	returns e to the n
floor(n)	rounds down to next integer
log(n)	returns natural logarithm of n
max(n,m)	returns greater of n and m
min(n,m)	returns lesser of n and m
pow(n,m)	returns n to the m
random()	returns random number between zero and one
round(n)	rounds to closest integer
sin(n)	returns sine of n
sqrt(n)	returns square root of n
tan(n)	returns tangent of n

Script 6.12 The Math object allows you to perform math operations on your page.

```
                       script
<HTML><HEAD><TITLE>Math Operations</TITLE>
<SCRIPT LANGUAGE="JavaScript">
<!--HIDE
function calculate(num) {
   with (document.forms[0]) {
      field1.value = Math.acos(num)
      field2.value = Math.cos(num)
      field3.value = Math.log(num)
      field4.value = Math.atan(num)
   }
}
//STOP HIDING-->
</SCRIPT></HEAD>
<BODY><H2><FORM>
Enter number:
<INPUT TYPE="text" VALUE="number"
→onChange=calculate(this.value)></H2>
<H3>arc cosine<INPUT TYPE="text" NAME="field1">
cosine<INPUT TYPE="text" NAME="field2">
log<INPUT TYPE="text" NAME="field3">
arc tangent<INPUT TYPE="text" NAME="field4">
</H3></FORM>
</BODY></HTML>
```

PERFORMING MATH OPERATIONS

The average user does not expect a web page to perform logarithmic operations with his input. But if you're creating a science page of any sort, you'll be glad you have the option. Math includes a number of methods (see Table 6.4) you can use to perform operations more sophisticated than basic arithmetic, as we've done in Script 6.12.

To perform math operations:

field2.value = Math.cos(num)

1.   Math

In your script, type **Math** to access the Math object.

2.   .cos

Type the name of the operation you want to perform. You can find a complete list of these in Table 6.4.

3.   (num)

Within parentheses, type the number that JavaScript should use in the operation or a variable which stores it.

4. field2.value =

Address the text field you want to use for display and assign it the result of your operation using the equals sign. If you perform an operation that does not yield a legal number, you will get **NaN**, which stands for "Not a Number," as the result.

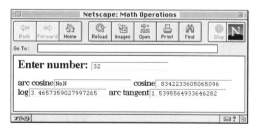

Figure 6.11 You can create a page that includes mathematical operations.

ROUNDING NUMBERS

You can use **parseInt()** (see page 81) to make an integer into a floating-point, but this just chops off the decimal places. For more precise rounding, you can use the three rounding methods accessed through **Math** (see Table 6.4). Script 6.13 demonstrates the different rounding methods.

To round numbers:

elements[2].value = Math.ceil(number)

1. Math

Type **Math** to address the Math object.

2. .ceil(   )

Type the name of the rounding technique you want to use. **Ceil()** always rounds up.

OR .floor(   )

You can use **floor()** to round down.

OR .round(   )

You can use **round()** to tell JavaScript to follow standard math rounding rules: anything above .5 is rounded up.

3. number

Within the parentheses, type the number you want JavaScript to round or a variable that stores it.

4. elements[2].value =

Using the equals sign, assign the rounded result to a text field or other element to display it (see page 52).

Script 6.13 JavaScript has a number of methods that round numbers.

```
<HTML>
<HEAD>
<TITLE>Rounding Numbers</TITLE>
<SCRIPT LANGUAGE="JavaScript">
<!--HIDE
function doRound(x) {
    var number=eval(x.value)
    with (document.forms[0]) {
        elements[1].value = Math.floor(number)
        elements[2].value = Math.ceil(number)
        elements[3].value = parseInt(number)
        elements[4].value = Math.round(number)
    }
}
//STOP HIDING-->
</SCRIPT></HEAD>
<BODY><FORM>
<H2>Enter a floating point number:</H2>
<INPUT TYPE="text" SIZE=10 onChange="doRound
→(this)">
with floor()<INPUT TYPE="text" SIZE=3>
with ceil()<INPUT TYPE="text" SIZE=3>
with parseInt()<INPUT TYPE="text" SIZE=3>
with round()<INPUT TYPE="text" SIZE=3>
</FORM></BODY>
</HTML>
```

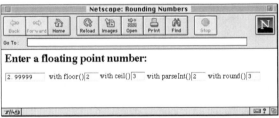

Figure 6.12 Each method of rounding uses different rules.

Script 6.14 The max method of Math returns the larger of two numerical arguments.

```
script
<HTML><HEAD><TITLE>Math Constants</TITLE>
<SCRIPT LANGUAGE="JavaScript">
<!--HIDE
var mess = new Array()
var str = ""
function splitIt(str) {
  mess = str.split(" ")
  var greatest = mess[0]
  for(var i=0;i<mess.length;i++) {
    greatest = Math.max(greatest,mess[i])
  }
  document.theForm.output.value = greatest
}
//STOP HIDING-->
</SCRIPT></HEAD>
<BODY><FORM NAME="theForm"><H2>
Enter numbers:
<INPUT TYPE="text" NAME="messy" SIZE=50
→onChange="order(this.value)">
<BR><BR>The largest number is
<INPUT TYPE="text" NAME="output">
</FORM></BODY></HTML>
```

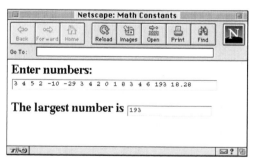

Figure 6.13 This script uses max() to compare the user's entries. It then displays the largest number in a text field.

COMPARING NUMBERS

If you ask the user to enter two numbers to be used by your script, you'll often need to determine which one is greater. You could use a conditional to achieve this, but it is much easier to take advantage of **min()** and **max()**. These return the smaller and larger of two numbers, respectively. Script 6.14 uses **max()** in place of a conditional (see page 66) to find the largest entered number.

To determine the largest number:

1. mess = str.split(" ")

   Within a function, split the user's text at the space character to divide it into individual numbers (see page 89). Assign this to a variable to work with it later.

2. var greatest = mess[0]

   Create a variable and use the equals sign to store the first entry in the new array of numbers. You will compare this against all of the others, so that **greatest** stores the largest number when the function is complete.

3. for(var i = 0; i < mess.length; i++) {

   Use a for loop to cycle through each element in the array (see page 74).

4. greatest = Math.max(greatest,mess[i]) }

   Math.max(   ) }

   Within the loop, type **Math.max** and add parentheses.

   greatest,mess[i]

   Type the name of your variable, a comma, and then the address of the current array entry. These two numbers are compared and the greater is kept. When the loop finishes **greatest** contains the largest of all of the entered numbers.

RANDOMLY SELECTED IMAGES

A randomly selected graphic makes your page more interesting. It helps to bring users back and make your page feel new. You can use JavaScript to select an image at random, as in Script 6.15.

To use randomly selected images:

1. Name your graphics files in numerical order (e.g. "1.gif", "2.gif").

2. document.write("<IMG SRC='" + Math.ceil (Math.random() * 4) + ".gif'>")

   document.write("<IMG SRC='" +
                          + ".gif'>")

   Use document.write() to write an image tag. Because the source attribute requires a string value, you must add quotation marks around your image name.

                                Math.ceil
   (   )

   Address the ceil method and add parentheses (see page 94). You should use this instead of round() to provide an equal chance of each image being selected.

    Math.random() * 4

   Tell JavaScript to generate a random number (see page 91) and multiply it by the number of images you are using.

Script 6.15 By rounding a random number and storing your image files by number, you can include random graphics on your page.

```
script
<HTML>
<HEAD><TITLE>Randomizing Graphics</TITLE>
</HEAD>
<BODY>
<SCRIPT LANGUAGE="JavaScript">
<!--HIDE
document.write("<IMG SRC='" + Math.ceil
→(Math.random() * 4) + ".gif'>")
//STOP HIDING-->
</SCRIPT>
<H2>This is Ted. He's your best friend.</H2>
</BODY>
</HTML>
```

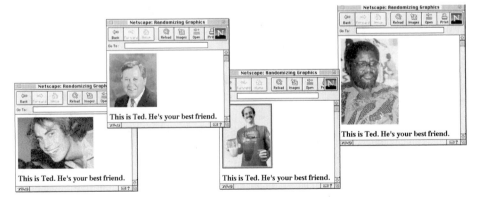

Figure 6.14 Math.random() can help you make friends.

WITHIN THE WINDOW

7

Table 7.1

window object (single window)	
PROPERTIES	**METHODS**
status string value of status message	alert() calls alert dialog
defaultStatus default value of status message	confirm() calls confirm dialog
	prompt() calls prompt dialog
EVENT HANDLERS	scroll() scrolls the window
onLoad loading finishes	setTimeout() pauses before execution
onUnload user leaves page	clearTimeout() clears timer
onError loading triggers error	

Everything you see in the browser window belongs to an object called **window**. Many of the commands you have learned, such as **alert()** and **confirm()**, are actually methods of this object. This means that most addresses could begin with **window** and a dot. Instead of forcing you to type this every time, JavaScript allows you to omit it.

This chapter covers the things you can do with one window. The properties, methods, and event handlers we will explain are listed in Table 7.1. JavaScript also allows you to work with multiple windows. Chapter 10 covers these techniques.

REACTING TO PAGE LOADING

Most event handlers respond to user actions on the page. **OnLoad** and **onUnload** differ in that they respond to the loading of the page itself. By using **onLoad** and **onUnload,** you can trigger a function when the page is finished downloading or when the user leaves the page. Script 7.1, for example, displays a thank you message when the page is complete.

If your script tries to access a part of the page while it is still loading, you will get an error message. To avoid this, you should use **onLoad** to trigger your script as soon as the page loads.

To react to the loading of a page:

```
<BODY onLoad="thanks()">
```

1. `<BODY              >`

Specify the HTML body tag.

2. `           onLoad`

Use the onLoad event handler to trigger your function when the page, including all images, finishes loading.

OR `           onUnload`

You can use **onUnload** to trigger a function when the user leaves the page by any means: clicking on a link, quitting the browser, or closing the window.

3. `              ="thanks()"`

Type the name of your function followed by parentheses. Assign it to the event handler with an equals sign.

Script 7.1 You can use onLoad to avoid script references to page elements not yet loaded.

```
<HTML>
<HEAD><TITLE>Load Example</TITLE>
<SCRIPT LANGUAGE="JavaScript">
<!--HIDE
function thanks () {
   document.forms[0].outfield.value = "Thank
   →you for your patience."
}
//STOP HIDING-->
</SCRIPT></HEAD>
<BODY onLoad="thanks()">
<IMG SRC="a.gif"><IMG SRC="b.gif">
<IMG SRC="c.gif"><IMG SRC="d.gif"><BR>
<FORM><INPUT TYPE="text" VALUE="Please wait for
→images to load..." SIZE=40 NAME="outfield">
</FORM></BODY></HTML>
```

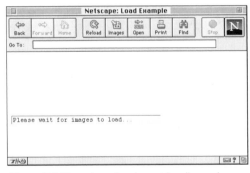

Figure 7.1 Here the onLoad event handler replaces the value of a text field when the page has finished loading.

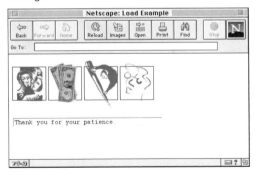

Script 7.2 You can use onerror to suppress error messages.

```
<HTML><HEAD><TITLE>Errors Example</TITLE>
<SCRIPT LANGUAGE="JavaScript">
<!--HIDE
var errors = new errorObjMaker()
var count = 0
function myError(msg,url,ln) {
  errors[count] = msg
  errors[count += 1] = ln
  count += 1
  return true
}
function errorObjMaker() {
}
function rubItIn() {
  var str = "MESSAGE \\ LINE\n\n"
  for (var i = 0;i < count; i++) {
    str += errors[i]
    str += (((i+1) % 2) == 0) ? "\n\n" : "\n"
  }
  document.forms[0].disp.value = str
}
window.onerror = myError
//STOP HIDING--> </SCRIPT></HEAD>
<BODY> <FORM>
<TEXTAREA onBlur="eval(this.value)"></TEXTAREA>
<BR><INPUT TYPE="button" VALUE="Try the code"
→onClick="rubItIn()"><BR>
<TEXTAREA NAME="disp"></TEXTAREA>
</FORM></BODY></HTML>
```

Figure 7.2 An error handling function can store error messages and display them upon request.

SUPPRESSING ERROR MESSAGES

Each time a JavaScript error occurs, the browser normally calls up an error alert describing it. Although these are useful for debugging, they can also be annoying. To avoid them you can either suppress all error messages or provide an error handling function. Script 7.2 replaces error alerts with a text field display.

You achieve this by assigning either **null** or a function to the onError event handler. Whenever JavaScript cannot understand a line of code, it triggers **onerror**. Because HTML does not recognize it, you must assign **onerror** within your script. This is the same technique used in Chapter 3 to reset an event handler (see page 41).

To suppress error messages:

1. window.onerror = myError

window.onerror

Address **onerror** within your script. Because you are not assigning it in an HTML tag, you must treat it as a property. Type **window** followed by a dot and then **onerror** in all lowercase.

= myError

Assign your error handling function to **onerror** with an equals sign. JavaScript will call it each time an error occurs.

OR = null

To ignore all errors, you can assign the keyword **null** to **onerror**.

2. function myError (msg, url, ln) {

Create a function to store the error information. Define it with three arguments: the error message, URL, and line number.

3. return true

Type **return true** in this function to tell Navigator to suppress the error alert.

Scrolling the User's Window

Web designers often need to encourage the user to scroll through a full page. With JavaScript you can bypass the user entirely, and make the window scroll on its own. Navigator 3.0 allows you to scroll the contents of the page exactly as if the user were clicking on the scroll bar's arrows (see Figure 7.3).

When you're working with **scroll()** you can pretend that there is a piece of graph paper over the full contents of the page. The lines on this paper are one pixel apart and are numbered from 0,0 at the top left corner of the page. When you give JavaScript the horizontal and vertical coordinates of a point on the grid, it scrolls the window to that point.

To scroll the user's window:

window.scroll(x, y)

1. window

Within your script, type **window** to address the current window.

2. .scroll(   )

Type a dot followed by **scroll** and parentheses to tell JavaScript that you want to scroll the page within the window.

3. x

Specify the number of pixels from the left side of the full page for JavaScript to scroll the window. Script 7.3 uses a for loop to scroll the window in ten pixel steps.

4. , y

Specify the number of pixels from the top of the full page for JavaScript to scroll the window.

Script 7.3 A for loop scrolls the window in ten-pixel increments.

```
<HTML><HEAD>
<SCRIPT LANGUAGE="JavaScript">
<!--HIDE
function doIt() {
   y = 0
   for (var x = 0; x <= 230; x += 10) {
     window.scroll(i,0)
   }
}
//STOP HIDING-->
</SCRIPT></HEAD>
<BODY>
<H3>A detail of the Sistine Chapel</H3>
<FORM><INPUT TYPE="button" VALUE="Turn your
→head" onClick="doIt()"></FORM>
<IMG SRC="creation.gif">
</BODY></HTML>
```

Figure 7.3 When the user clicks the button, JavaScript scrolls the window the window to the right.

Script 7.4 By setting the status or defaultStatus property, you can display messages in the window's status bar.

```
<HTML>
<HEAD>
<TITLE>Status Example</TITLE>
</HEAD>
<BODY onLoad="defaultStatus = 'Welcome to my
→page; enjoy!'">
<H1>My Home Page</H1>
</BODY>
</HTML>
```

DISPLAYING A STATUS BAR MESSAGE

The gray area at the bottom of a browser window is known as the status bar. In this space the browser displays information about its progress in loading documents and images.

Customizing the text in the status bar is one of the most frequent uses of JavaScript. You achieve it with **defaultStatus** and **status**. Text assigned to **status** displays immediately, but disappears the next time the browser displays a message. You will generally use **status** to associate messages with user events, such as moving over a link.

DefaultStatus sets the default value of the status text for as long as the page is loaded. You can use this to display a message which doesn't change and is visible when no message would normally appear, as we've done with Script 7.4.

To display a message in the status bar:

```
<BODY onLoad="defaultStatus='Welcome to
my page; enjoy!'">
```

1. `<BODY onLoad="defaultStatus
">`

Within the body tag's onLoad event handler (see page 97), type **defaultStatus** to signal that you want to replace the default text for the status bar (see Figure 7.4).

OR `<A HREF="URL" onMouseOver="status
">`

To display a message when the user moves over a link, assign **status** to the onMouseOver event handler for the desired link (see page 108).

2. `='Welcome to
my page; enjoy!'`

Use the equals sign to assign the desired message.

Figure 7.4 You can use defaultStatus to display a message when none would normally appear.

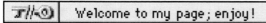

INSERTING A PAUSE

If you wanted to cycle through a set of images, you might write a command for each image change or use a for loop. In either case, however, the images would change so fast that you would never see them. In situations like this, you need to slow JavaScript down with a pause.

SetTimeout() makes JavaScript wait the number of milliseconds you specify before reading the code you give it. JavaScript does not sit idle while it's waiting however, it continues reading the rest of your script.

You can give the user the ability to stop the timer with **clearTimeout()**.

To insert a pause:

1. var timer = null

At the start of your script, declare a global variable to store the timer ID.

2. <BODY onLoad="timer = setTimeout('move()', 5000)

timer =

Where you want the timer to begin, type the name of your timer variable and **=** to store the timer ID.

setTimeout(   )

Specify the setTimeout method to tell JavaScript to insert a pause.

'move()'

Within quotation marks specify the code to be executed after the pause. Script 7.5 pauses before moving the user to a new URL.

, 5000

Type a comma and then the number of milliseconds that you want to delay.

3. onClick="clearTimeout(timer)"

Use **clearTimeout()** with the timer ID if you want to stop the timer.

Script 7.5 SetTimeout() makes JavaScript wait before reading the code you specify.

```
<HTML>
<HEAD><TITLE>setTimeout() Example</TITLE>
<SCRIPT LANGUAGE="JavaScript">
<!--HIDE
var timer = null
function move() {
    window.location = 'http://www.ted.and
    →.jeremy.server'
//STOP HIDING-->
</SCRIPT></HEAD>
<BODY onLoad="timer=setTimeout
→('move()',5000)">
<CENTER><H1>Attention!</H1></CENTER>
<H3>Ted and Jeremy's JavaScript site has moved
to a new URL. Please change your bookmarks to
<H2>http://www.ted.and.jeremy.server</H2>
We'll bring you there in just a moment.</H3>
<BR><FORM>
<INPUT TYPE="button" VALUE="No! I refuse to
→leave!" onClick="clearTimeout(timer)">
</BODY></HTML>
```

Figure 7.5 The script waits five seconds before moving the user to a new location. If she clicks the button, it clears the timer.

Script 7.6 You can display a scrolling message in the status bar which moves from right to left.

```
<HTML><HEAD><TITLE>Scroll Example</TITLE>
<SCRIPT LANGUAGE="JavaScript">
<!--HIDE
var nspaces = 150
var timer
var msg = ""
function scrollMaster() {
  clearTimeout(timer)
  msg = "Welcome to World Wide Power
  →Corporation!"
  for (var i = 0; i < nspaces; i++) {
    msg = " " + msg
  }
  scrollMe()
}
function scrollMe() {
    window.status = msg
    msg = msg.substring(1, msg.length) +
    →msg.substring(0,1)
    timer = setTimeout("scrollMe()", 150)
}
//STOP HIDING--></SCRIPT></HEAD>
<BODY><FORM>
<INPUT TYPE="button" VALUE="Display" onClick=
→"scrollMaster()">
</FORM></BODY></HTML>
```

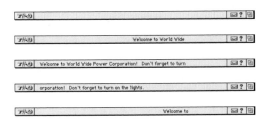

Figure 7.6 A scrolling status message can display a message longer than the status bar.

DISPLAYING A SCROLLING MESSAGE

You can display a message in the status bar with the technique on page 101. If you want to get a little fancier, however, you can make this message scroll. You'll also want to do this if you have more text than would normally fit in the status bar.

To display a scrolling status message:

1. function scrollMaster () {

At the beginning of your script, define a master function to prepare the message for display.

2. msg = "Welcome to World Wide Power Corporation!"

Use the equals sign to assign your message to the variable **msg**.

3. for (var i = 0; i < nspaces ; i++) {
msg = " " + msg }

To make the message begin at the right, use a for loop to insert a large number of spaces before it (see page 74).

4. scrollMe()

After the loop is complete, call **scrollMe()**.

5. window.status = msg

Within the scrolling function, use = to assign the current value of the message to the status bar each time JavaScript cycles through the function.

6. msg = msg.substring(1, msg.length) +
msg.substring(0,1)

In this line, the + moves the first character of the string to its end to create the scroll effect (see page 23). As this occurs repeatedly, the text moves from right to left. This technique ensures that the message will scroll repeatedly.

7. timer = setTimeout("scrollMe()", 150)

Use **setTimeout()** to slow down the scrolling (see page 102). It issues a delayed call to the scrolling function.

CHANGING THE COLORS OF A PAGE

Everything that you create in your HTML document belongs to an object called **document**. This includes the links, images and forms on your page as subobjects. It also lets you access the color attributes that you define in the body tag. You can find a listing of the color properties in Table 7.2.

You can set the color properties by assigning them a color name or hexadecimal color code. Most of these changes immediately alter the coloring of the page. Some, however, such as foreground color, do not work at all in the current version of Navigator (see Figure 7.7).

To change the colors of a page:

document.bgColor = "silver"

1. document

Type **document** to address the current HTML document.

2. .bgColor

Type a dot followed by the name of the color property you want to change (see Table 7.2).

3. = "silver"

Use the equals sign to assign the new color to the property. Specify the color as either a hexadecimal value or one of Navigator's named color references. You must surround these with quotation marks.

Table 7.2

document object (single document)	
COLOR PROPERTIES	**PROPERTIES**
alinkColor color of link when clicked	cookie string stored on client machine
bgColor color of background	title title of page
fgColor color of text	referrer URL of calling document
linkColor color of links	
vlinkColor color of followed links	lastModified date of last modification

Script 7.7 You can use the color properties to change the coloring of your page.

```
<HTML><HEAD><TITLE>Color Example</TITLE>
<SCRIPT LANGUAGE="JavaScript">
<!--HIDE
function changeOne () {
    document.bgColor = "white"
    document.fgColor = "black"
}
function changeTwo () {
    document.bgColor = "silver"
    document.fgColor = "white"
}
//STOP HIDING-->
</SCRIPT></HEAD>
<BODY><FORM>
<H2>What is your favorite color?</H2>
<INPUT TYPE="button" VALUE="white"
→onClick="changeOne()">
<INPUT TYPE="button" VALUE="silver"
→onClick="changeTwo()">
</FORM></BODY></HTML>
```

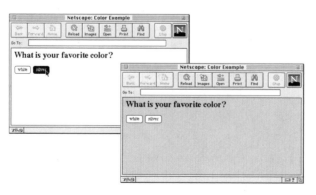

Figure 7.7 When the user clicks a button, the script assigns new background and foreground colors, but only the background color changes.

Script 7.8 The referrer property returns the URL of the calling page.

```
                    script
<HTML>
<HEAD><TITLE>document.referrer Example
</TITLE></HEAD>
<BODY><SCRIPT LANGUAGE="JavaScript">
<!--HIDE
function getRefName() {
  var ref=document.referrer
  var refTwo= ref.split("//")
  var theHost=refTwo[1].split("/")
  return theHost[0]
}
document.write("<H2>")
if (document.referrer != "") {
  document.write("Thanks for coming to my page
  →from " + getRefName())
} else {
  document.write("You came here all by
  →yourself.")
}
document.write("</H2>")
//STOP HIDING-->
</SCRIPT></BODY></HTML>
```

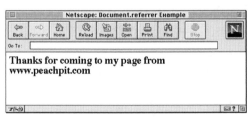

Figure 7.8 With the referrer property you can alter the content of your page depending on whether the user arrived through a link.

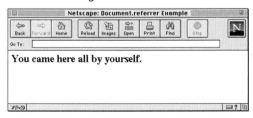

DETERMINING THE PREVIOUS URL

When the user follows a hypertext link to your page, the linking page is described as the referrer. You can access this page's URL through the referrer property. If the user came to your page through a bookmark or entry in the location field, **referrer** contains a null string ("").

If your site has multiple pages, you can use **referrer** to check whether a page has been reached through an internal or external link, and use a conditional (see page 66) to change the content accordingly.

To determine the previous URL:

1. if (document.referrer != "") {
document.write("Thanks for coming to my page from " + getRefName())

document

Within your function, type **document** to address the current page.

.referrer

Type a dot followed by **referrer** to address the referrer property. This stores the URL of the page which linked to yours.

!= ""

To be sure that the user reached your site directly, use **!=** (see page 68) to test if **referrer** contains a URL.

if (   ) {
document.write("Thanks for coming to my page from " + getRefName())

Use this as the condition of an if statement (see page 67). Enter the statements to be used if the user has arrived through a link within the braces. Script 7.8 uses a function to isolate the host name.

2. } else { document.write("You came here all by yourself." }

Type **else** followed by braces containing the statements you want to be used if the user reached your page directly.

TESTING THE NUMBER OF ANCHORS

You can use JavaScript to work with both links and anchors. JavaScript stores these in two arrays: links[ ] and anchors[ ].

You can determine how many anchors there are on the page, but you cannot change them in any way. However, you can use JavaScript to change any attribute of your links. The link properties, listed in Table 7.3, include several components of the destination URL, such as its port, host, and path.

To determine the number of anchors on a page:

document.anchors.length

1. document.anchors

   Within your script, type **document** followed by a dot and **anchors** to address JavaScript's array of the anchors on your page.

2. .length

   Type a dot followed by **length** to access the number of anchor tags on the page. Script 7.9 puts this in a document.write command to display the information on the page.

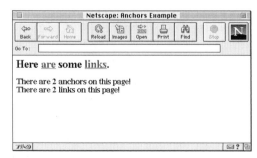

Figure 7.9 Both the anchors and links arrays include a length property, which stores the number of tags on the page.

Table 7.3

link object	hypertext link
PROPERTIES (LINK OBJECT)	**EVENT HANDLERS**
hash anchor portion of URL	onClick user clicks link
host hostname and port portion of URL	onMouseOver mouse moves over link
hostname host and domain	onMouseOut mouse moves off link
href entire URL	
pathname document's directory path	**PROPERTIES (LINKS ARRAY)**
port port number on server	length number of links in document
protocol beginning of URL to colon (e.g., http:)	
search query information	
target target frame of link	

Script 7.9 JavaScript stores a page's links and anchors in arrays.

```
script

<HTML>
<HEAD><TITLE>Anchors Example</TITLE></HEAD>
<BODY><H2>
<A NAME="here">Here</A>
<A HREF="#some">are</A>
<A NAME="some">some</A>
<A HREF="#here">links</A>.</H2><H3>
<SCRIPT LANGUAGE="JavaScript">
<!--HIDE
document.write("There are " + document.anchors
→.length + " anchors on this page!<BR>")
document.write("There are " + document.links
→.length + " links on this page!")
//STOP HIDING-->
</SCRIPT></H3></BODY></HTML>
```

Script 7.10 By returning false to onClick you can prevent the user from following a link.

```
<HTML>
<HEAD>
<TITLE>Return False</TITLE>
</HEAD>
<BODY>
<CENTER>
<A HREF="http://www.another.woman.com" onClick=
→"return confirm('Do you want to leave and
→have me hate you forever?')">
<IMG SRC="leaveme.gif">
</A>
</CENTER>
</BODY>
</HTML>
```

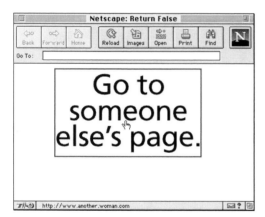

Figure 7.10 If the user chooses No in the dialog box, the location does not change.

CONFIRMING A LINK

Sometimes users don't know whether a link goes to another page on your site or to another site altogether. To prevent accidental exits from your site, you may want to confirm external links that might be confusing.

You can respond to a click on a link with **onClick**, but this normally does not stop the browser from following the link. To prevent the location change from taking effect, you must return **false** to **onClick**, as in Script 7.16. You saw this technique used with the reset and submit elements on page 59.

To confirm a link to another site:

> `<A HREF="http://www.another.woman.com" onClick="return confirm('Do you want to leave and have me hate you forever?')">`

1. `<A HREF="http://www.another.woman.com" >`

   Within your HTML document, create a link to the desired location.

2. `onClick=" "`

   Within the link tag, insert the onClick event handler, which will respond to a click on the link.

3. `return`

   Precede your function call with **return**. This enables the value returned by your function to prevent the browser from following the link.

4. `confirm('Do you want to leave and have me hate you forever?')`

   Type the name of a function which yields a **true** or **false** response and follow it with parentheses. If it returns **true**, the browser will go to the new location; if it returns **false**, the browser will stay at the current page. Because **confirm()** returns the appropriate values, you can use it to display your message.

RESPONDING TO MOUSE MOVEMENT

You can make your page more friendly to the user by providing feedback as the mouse moves over images and links.

You do this by responding to mouse location with **onMouseOver** and **onMouseOut**. When the user moves onto a link, she triggers **onMouseOver**. You will often use this to display information in the window status bar, as described on page 101.

Navigator 3.0 has added **onMouseOut**, which responds when the user moves off a link. Script 7.11 uses both of these event handlers to time the user's actions with **setTimeout()** (see page 102).

To respond to mouse movement:

```
<A HREF="#" onMouseOver="startTime()"
onMouseOut="clearTimeout(time)">
```

1. `<A HREF="#" onMouseOver`

   `>`

   Place the onMouseOver event handler within the HTML tag for the desired link.

2. `="startTime()"`

   Type = followed by a call to your function in quotation marks. **OnMouseOver** will trigger this function when the user moves over the link. Script 7.11 uses this technique to start a timer.

3. onMouseOut

   Add **onMouseOut** to your link tag to respond when the user moves off the link.

4. `="clearTimeout(time)"`

   Assign your desired function call to **onMouseOut** with the equals sign. Script 7.11 clears the timer set with **onMouse-Over** when the user moves off the link (see Figure 7.11).

Script 7.11 By using setTimeout(), you can make onMouseOver and onMouseOut time the user's actions.

```
<HTML>
<HEAD><TITLE>Mouse Events Example</TITLE>
<SCRIPT LANGAGE="JavaScript">
<!--HIDE
var time=null
function startTime() {
   time=setTimeout("alert('Quit stalling.
   →Just click it!')", 2000)
}
//STOP HIDING-->
</SCRIPT></HEAD><BODY>
<A HREF="#" onMouseOver="startTime()"
→onMouseOut="clearTimeout(time)">
Cool Link!</A>
</BODY></HTML>
```

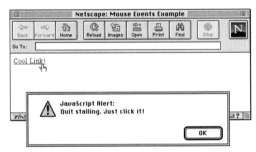

Figure 7.11 The alert pops up if the user stays on the link for two seconds.

Script 7.12 You can create a multi-purpose link by changing its destination in your script.

```
<HTML>
<HEAD><TITLE>Changing a Link</TITLE>
<SCRIPT LANGUAGE="JavaScript">
<!--HIDE
function changeIt(newLoc) {
   document.links[0].href=newLoc
}
//STOP HIDING-->
</SCRIPT></HEAD>
<BODY>
<A HREF="http://www.peachpit.com">
Cool Link!</A>
<FORM><H3>Choose your favorite topic:<BR>
<INPUT TYPE="radio" NAME="choices" onClick=
→"changeIt('http://www.kant.com')">
Philosophy<BR>
<INPUT TYPE="radio" NAME="choices" onClick=
→"changeIt('http://www.world.power.corp.com')">
Energy/Imperialism<BR>
<INPUT TYPE="radio" NAME="choices" onClick=
→"changeIt('http://www.cummings.com')">Poetry
</H3></BODY></HTML>
```

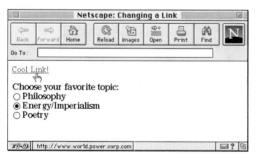

Figure 7.12 The user's radio selection changes the href property of a link.

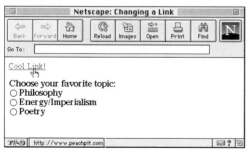

CHANGING A LINK'S REFERENCE

Normally, if you want to provide the user with links to several URLs, you create a number of link tags. You can do the same thing more efficiently by using a single link. Script 7.12, for example, lets the user choose what kind of link she is interested in and alters a single link's destination accordingly.

You can do this by modifying parts of the location that JavaScript stores for the link.

To change a link's reference:

1. function changeIt(newLoc) {

Define a function to change the reference of a link. Give it one argument, which will store the new URL.

2. document.links[0].href = newLoc }

document.links

Within your script, type **document** followed by **.links** to address the links array (see page 29).

[0]

Type the index number of the desired link within brackets.

.href

Type the name of one of the link location properties (see Table 7.3). **Href** stores the full URL.

= newLoc }

Use an equals sign to assign the new destination for the link.

3. <INPUT TYPE="radio" NAME="choices" onClick="changeIt('http://www.kant.com')">

Within the body of your HTML document, create the desired button or select list. Use an event handler to trigger your function and pass it the new URL for the link (see page 38).

PROVIDING HELP FOR THE USER

Your browser normally displays the destination of a link in the status bar when the you move over it. To provide more helpful information, you can script your links to display messages in the status bar, as in Script 7.13.

To do this, you assign a display function to **onMouseOver**. When the user moves over the link, the display function puts a help message in the status bar. You do not need to use **onMouseOut** to reset the status message when the user leaves the link.

To provide help for the user:

```
<A HREF="#" onMouseOver= "
window.status = 'a book is a large collection
of pages bound together.'; return true">
```

1. `<A HREF="#" onMouseOver= "`
              `"`

Insert **onMouseOver** in the desired link tag to respond when the mouse moves over the link (see page 108).

2. window.status

Within the event handler, address the status bar text (see page 101).

3.   = 'a book is a large collection of pages bound together.'

Use the equals sign to assign the desired help message. This displays it in the status bar at the bottom of the window.

4.   ; return true

Type a semicolon to include a second statement. Follow this with **return true**. You must do this whenever a status message is triggered by **onMouseOver** in order for the message to be displayed.

Script 7.13 The status bar displays information about the links on the page.

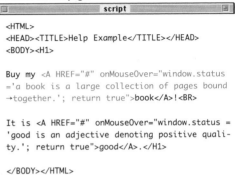

```
<HTML>
<HEAD><TITLE>Help Example</TITLE></HEAD>
<BODY><H1>

Buy my <A HREF="#" onMouseOver="window.status
='a book is a large collection of pages bound
→together.'; return true">book</A>!<BR>

It is <A HREF="#" onMouseOver="window.status =
'good is an adjective denoting positive quali-
ty.'; return true">good</A>.</H1>

</BODY></HTML>
```

Figure 7.13 Context-sensitive help provides information about links or other elements when the user moves over them.

IMAGES AND IMAGE MAPS

8

Image object	
PROPERTIES (OBJECT)	**EVENT HANDLERS**
border border size in pixels	onAbort image loading stops
complete true if fully loaded	onError error encountered in loading image
height image height in pixels	
hspace horizontal margin	onLoad image loading completed
lowsrc source file of preliminary image	
	PROPERTIES (ARRAY)
src image source file	length number of images in document
name value of name attribute	
vspace vertical margin	
width image width in pixels	

Beginning with Navigator 3.0, JavaScript can control the images on a web page. This new ability has made JavaScript more popular and could quickly become its most common use.

In this chapter, you will learn how to work with images through the items listed in Table 8.1. You can use these to do things like change an image when the user moves the mouse over it and create simple animations for your page.

As you go through the scripts involving images, you will find that we frequently define images as links to make them more scriptable. This technique allows your script to respond to mouse movement over an image.

DETERMINING IMAGE ATTRIBUTES

HTML restricts what you can do with the layout of a page once it has loaded, so you can't change most of an image's attributes. You can, however, read this information and respond to it.

To determine an image's HTML attributes:

> alert(document.images[0].height)

1. document

Address the document object anywhere in your script.

2. .images

Type a dot followed by **images** to address the images object. This array contains all of the images on the page (see page 29).

3. [0]

Enter the image's index number within braces to specify a particular image within the array.

4. .height

Address one of the properties listed in Table 8.1. **Height** stores the vertical size of your image in pixels (see Figure 8.1).

5. alert(   )

You can test this value or use it for display. Script 8.1 alerts a variety of image properties.

Script 8.1 You can change an image's source (see page 118), but anything involving its layout is read-only

```
<HTML><HEAD>
<TITLE>Accessing Image Attributes</TITLE>
</HEAD>
<BODY>
<IMAGE NAME="Sistine Chapel, detail" SRC=
→"create.gif" ALIGN=left HSPACE= 20 BORDER=3>
<SCRIPT LANGUAGE="JavaScript">
<!--HIDE
alert("The image border is " +
→document.images[0].border + ".\n" +
→"The image height is " +
→document.images[0].height + ".\n" +
→"The image name is " +
→document.images[0].name + ".\n" +
→"The image vertical margin is " +
→document.images[0].vspace + ".\n" +
→"The image horizontal margin is " +
→document.images[0].hspace + ".\n" +
→"The image width is " +
→document.images[0].width + ".\n")
//STOP HIDING--></SCRIPT>
<BR><BR><H3>Look at the pretty picture.</H3>
</BODY></HTML>
```

Figure 8.1 An alert displays the HTML attributes of an image.

Script 8.2 The complete property stores false if the image is in the process of loading.

```
                    script
<HTML>
<HEAD><TITLE>Complete Example</TITLE></HEAD>
<BODY><CENTER>
<IMG SRC="hand.gif" NAME="picture">
<BR><FORM>
<INPUT TYPE="text" VALUE="Please wait for the
→image to load..." SIZE=45 NAME="outfield">
</FORM></CENTER>
<SCRIPT LANGUAGE="JavaScript">
<!--HIDE
if (!document.picture.complete) {
   document.forms[0].outfield.value = "The
   →image is loading..."
   setTimeout("checkEm()", 100)
} else {
   document.forms[0].outfield.value = "Thank
   →you for your patience."
//STOP HIDING-->
</SCRIPT></BODY></HTML>
```

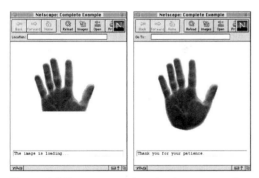

Figure 8.2 Text messages describe the progress of image loading.

REACTING TO IMAGE LOADING

Depending on the user's modem connection, he may have a long wait before he can see the images on your page. You can use JavaScript to display a message while the user waits. You do this by testing **complete**, a property of each image.

To check if an image is loading:

1. if (!document.picture.complete) {

if (   ) {

Create a conditional within your script (see page 66) to test whether the image is still loading.

!

Type ! so that you can trigger a message while the user is waiting, e.g. **complete** is not true. See page 69 for an explanation of the logical operators. Script 8.2 displays a message while the image is loading.

document.picture

Address the image to be tested either by name or by its index number in **images[ ]** (see page 29).

.complete

Address the image's complete property. Its value is **false** only while the image is in the process of loading. **Complete** stores **true** before an image begins loading and once it has finished loading.

2. document.forms[0].outfield.value = "The image is loading..."

Type the statements you want to trigger once the image starts loading. Script 8.2 displays a message in a text field.

REACTING TO IMAGE LOADING

If you want to change an image's source (see page 116) every five seconds, it would be silly to start the timer before the image has finished downloading. If your script works with images, you should be sure to delay it until the image is on the user's screen.

There are three techniques for testing whether images have loaded. You can use **complete** to trigger a part of your script when loading begins (see page 113). You can use the window's **onLoad** to react once all images on the page have loaded (see page 97). Or you can use a particular image's **onLoad** to react when it finishes loading.

To react to a completed image load:

<IMG SRC="a.gif" onLoad="display()">

1. **<IMG SRC="a.gif"   >**

   Define an image and assign it a source with an image tag.

2. **   onLoad=**

   Within the tag, type **onLoad** to react when the image finishes loading. See page 31 for an explanation of event handlers.

3. **   ="display()"**

   Use the equals sign to assign a function to **onLoad** that needs the image to be visible for it to work correctly. Script 8.3, for example, fills in information about each image as it appears.

Script 8.3 JavaScript triggers onLoad when an image finishes loading.

```
<HTML>
<HEAD><TITLE>onLoad Example</TITLE>
<SCRIPT LANGUAGE="JavaScript">
<!--HIDE
function display(msg,which) {
    document.theForm.elements[which].value = msg
}
//STOP HIDING-->
</SCRIPT></HEAD>
<BODY><FORM NAME="theForm">
<INPUT TYPE="text" SIZE=12>
<IMG SRC="a.gif" ALIGN="middle"
→onLoad="display('Reviews Page',0)"><BR>
<INPUT TYPE="text" SIZE=12>
<IMG SRC="b.gif" ALIGN="middle"
→onLoad="display('Finance Page',1)"><BR>
<INPUT TYPE="text" SIZE=12>
<IMG SRC="c.gif" ALIGN="middle"
→onLoad="display('News Page',2)"><BR>
</FORM></BODY></HTML>
```

Figure 8.3 The script displays a message with each image when it is done loading.

Script 8.4 JavaScript triggers onAbort when the user stops an image load.

```
<HTML>
<HEAD><TITLE>Reacting to Cancellation</TITLE>
<SCRIPT LANGUAGE="JavaScript">
<!--HIDE
function difftLink() {
    if (confirm("Sorry. I guess my images are
    →just too big for your puny modem. Will you
    →at least look at my text-only page?") ==
    →true) {
        window.location.pathname="/puny.htm"
    }
}
//STOP HIDING-->
</SCRIPT></HEAD>
<BODY><IMG SRC="mich.gif" onAbort=
→"difftLink()">
</BODY></HTML>
```

Figure 8.4 If the user stops an image load that's taking too long, you can offer to bring her to a text page.

Responding to an Image Abort

Anyone who's browsed the Web over regular telephone lines has experienced the frustration of waiting for an image to load. If you're designing a page with lots of graphics, you should respond to the needs of users with slow connections.

If a user decides that an image isn't worth waiting for, she'll hit the stop button. You can use **onAbort** to respond to this situation. Script 8.4 asks the user who stops an image load if she would like to move to a text-only page.

To respond to an image abort:

1. function difftLink() {

Define a function that will respond to the user's image abort.

2. if (confirm("Will you at least look at my text-only page?") == true) {

if (
) {

Type **if** to create a conditional (see page 67). You can follow { with any statements. Script 8.4 moves the window to a new URL (see page 149).

confirm("Will you at least look at my text-only page?") == true

Use the confirm command (see page 15) and == **true** as the condition (see page 68). JavaScript will only read the following statements if the user answers Yes.

3. <IMG SRC="mich.gif" onAbort="difftLink()">

<IMG SRC="mich.gif"   >

Define an image and assign it a source with an image tag.

onAbort="difftLink()"

Within the tag, type **onAbort** to react if the user stops the image load. Use the equals sign to assign your function to it.

CHANGING AN IMAGE

You can use JavaScript to change the images on your page. Script 8.5, for example, switches the graphic every four seconds to make the page more interesting.

Normally, when you change an image source, the user has to wait for the new image to download. By using the Image constructor, however, you can preload an image to the cache and then display it immediately.

To change an image:

1. var imageOne = new Image()

var imageOne =

Within your script, define a variable which will store your preloaded image.

new

Type **new** to tell JavaScript that you are creating an instance (see page 34).

Image()

Specify the Image constructor and follow it with parentheses. This creates an empty image object.

2. imageOne.src = "lycos.gif"

imageOne.src

Address the source of your new image by typing its variable name and **.src**.

= "lycos.gif"

Use **=** to assign a source to your image. This assignment triggers the loading of the image into the cache.

3. document.images[0].src = "lycos.gif"

document.images[0].src

Address the source of an image you have defined in your HTML.

= "lycos.gif"

To change the image, assign the image you have preloaded to this image source.

Script 8.5 You can replace a displayed image with a preloaded one instantly.

```
<HTML>
<HEAD><TITLE>Image Instances Example</TITLE>
<SCRIPT LANGUAGE="JavaScript">
<!--HIDE
var imageOne = new Image()
imageOne.src = "lycos.gif"
function change() {
    document.images[0].src = "lycos.gif"
    document.links[0].href="http://www.lycos.com"
}
setTimeout("change()",4000)
//STOP HIDING-->
</SCRIPT></HEAD>
<BODY>
<IMAGE SRC="inktomi.gif" >
<A HREF=http://www.hotbot.com>
search engine</A>
</HTML>
```

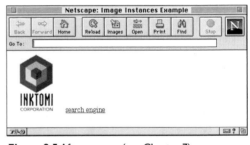

Figure 8.5 After a pause (see Chapter 7), a preloaded image replaces the first.

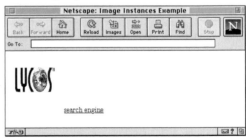

Script 8.6 With each click, the image source changes.

```
<HTML>
<HEAD><TITLE>Changing Images</TITLE>
<SCRIPT LANGUAGE="JavaScript">
<!--HIDE
var counter = 0
function changer() {
   counter += 1
   if (counter == 4) {
      counter = 0
   }
   document.images[0].src = counter + ".gif"
}
//STOP HIDING-->
</SCRIPT></HEAD>
<BODY>
<A HREF="#" onClick="changer()">
<IMAGE SRC="0.gif" BORDER=0></A>
</BODY></HTML>
```

Figure 8.6 By defining an image as a link, you can use onClick to change its source.

Triggering an Image Change

You can make any user event trigger an image change. You do this with the technique introduced on the previous page, assigning a new source to the image.

When you trigger such a change, be sure to check that the new and old images are the same size. If the new image has a different pixel height or width, JavaScript will automatically scale it.

To trigger an image change with an event:

1. Name your image files in numerical order (e.g., "0.gif", "1.gif").

2. var counter = 0

   Define a global counter variable.

3. counter += 1

   Within a function, type the name of your counter and +=1 to add one to it. See page 24 for more about the assignment operators.

4. if (counter == 4) { counter = 0 }

   Use a conditional (see page 67) to set your counter back to zero once it reaches the last image.

5. document.images[0].src = counter + ".gif"

   document.images[0].src

   Address the source of the image you want to change. Script 8.6 works with the first image on the page.

   = counter + ".gif"

   Use = to assign to the image source the name of your counter variable plus the string ".gif".

6. <A HREF="#" onClick="changer()">

   Within the link tag for the desired image, assign your image replacement function to an event handler (see page 32). Script 8.6 uses a click.

CREATING AN INTERACTIVE BUTTON

Have you ever noticed how the buttons in most programs appear to be pressed while your mouse is clicking on them? Software companies try to design their buttons to look more realistic, as if you're actually pressing a physical button. With JavaScript, you can add similar interactive buttons to your page to make it more friendly to the user.

You can create interactive buttons by using the mouse position event handlers and the image source.

To create an interactive button:

1. var down = new Image()

Within your script, use the Image constructor (see page 116) to create a new image.

2. down.src = "buttonDown.gif"

Type the variable name of your new image followed by **.src=** and the name of your image to preload it into the cache. Script 8.7 uses an image of a pressed button.

3. <A HREF="#" onMouseOver="document.images[0].src = down.src" onMouseOut = "document.images[0].src = 'up.gif'">

<A HREF="#"
                    >

Create an image link on your page.

          onMouseOver=

Type **onMouseOver=** to respond when the user moves over the image (see page 108).

                  "document.
images[0].src = down.src"

Address the image's source and assign it your image variable followed by **.src**.

               onMouseOut =
"document.images[0].src = 'up.gif'"

Use **onMouseOut** to reassign the original image when the user moves off the link.

Script 8.7 You can change an image when the user moves over it, and change it back when he moves off.

```
<HTML>
<HEAD><TITLE>Button Example</TITLE>
<SCRIPT LANGUAGE="JavaScript">
<!--HIDE
var down = new Image()
down.src = "buttonDown.gif"
//STOP HIDING-->
</SCRIPT></HEAD>
<BODY><CENTER>
<H1>WELCOME</H1>
<H2>You have reached the first page, to move
on, press the next button.</H2>
<A HREF="#" onMouseOver="document.images[0].src
→= down.src" onMouseOut="document.images[0]
→.src = 'up.gif'">
<IMG SRC="up.gif" BORDER=0 ALIGN="right">
</A></BODY></HTML>
```

Figure 8.7 Interactive buttons change their shading to look more like real buttons.

Script 8.8 To create a JavaScript animation, you can assign each new image to the same image source.

```
script
<HTML>
<HEAD><TITLE>JavaScript Animation</TITLE>
<SCRIPT LANGUAGE="JavaScript">
<!--HIDE
var counter = 0
var timer
var imgs = new Array()
for (var i = 1; i < 7; i++) {
   imgs[i] = new Image()
   imgs[i].src = i + ".gif"
}
function animate() {
   counter = (counter < 6) ? (counter + 1) : 0
   document.anim.src = imgs[counter].src
   timer=setTimeout("animate()", 100)
}
//STOP HIDING-->
</SCRIPT></HEAD>
<BODY onLoad="animate()"><FORM>
<IMAGE SRC="1.gif" NAME="anim">
<INPUT TYPE="button VALUE="STOP"
→onClick="clearTimeout(timer)"
</FORM></BODY></HTML>
```

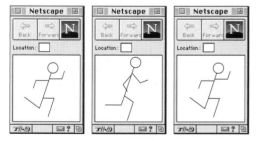

Figure 8.8 By displaying images in rapid succession you can create the illusion of life.

CREATING A JAVASCRIPT ANIMATION

You can choose from a number of ways to put animations on your web page, including segmented GIFs, Shockwave movies, and Java applets. JavaScript is useful as a means of animation because you can easily make it interactive. Script 8.8, for example, includes a stop button.

Using the Image constructor (see page 116), you can preload all of your images. If you do this, the animation will run smoothly from the beginning.

To create a JavaScript animation:

1. var imgs = new Array()

Use the Array constructor discussed on page 131 to create a set of new images. As in Script 8.8 you can then use a for loop (see page 74) with the Image constructor to preload your images.

2. counter = (counter < 6) ? (counter + 1) : 0

counter = (counter < 6) ?

Within a function, assign a conditional expression (see page 72) to a global counter variable. Type **counter <** and the number of images in your animation as the condition.

(counter + 1) : 0

If the counter has not reached the last image, assign it **counter + 1**. Type **: 0** to assign zero and reset the counter when it reaches the last image.

3. document.anim.src = imgs[counter].src

Assign the image its next source, using **counter** as the index number of your array,

4. timer = setTimeout("animate()", 100)

Use **setTimeout()** to slow down the animation (see page 102). Script 8.8 saves the timer ID in a variable so that the user can stop the animation.

MOVEMENT OVER AN IMAGE MAP

You create a client-side image map in HTML by using map tags. Within the map tags you put area tags, which define the different links in the image. With Navigator 3.0, you can use JavaScript to work with client-side maps.

Because each map area is essentially a special type of link, you can access areas through links[ ] (see page 106). Areas, however, can't respond to onClick.

To react to movement over an image map:

1. <MAP NAME="istanbulmap">

Signal the beginning of an image map by putting the map tag in your HTML document.

2. <AREA COORDS="298,129,507,158" HREF ="where.htm" onMouseOver="theForm.out .value='Make Reservations'">

<AREA   >

Place an area tag after your map tag.

COORDS="298,129,507,158"

Type **COORDS=** and assign the corner-points of an area.

HREF ="where.htm"

Type **HREF=** and assign your area the URL you want it to link to.

onMouseOver="theForm.out .value='Make Reservations'"

Assign the desired code to **onMouseOver** (see page 108). Script 8.9 displays a text message.

3. </MAP>

Type **</MAP>** to end the map definition.

4. <IMG SRC="img" USEMAP="#myMap">

Within the tag for the map image, type **USEMAP="#** and the name you have given your map followed by a quotation mark.

Script 8.9 You can now use JavaScript with client-side image maps.

```
<HTML><HEAD><TITLE>Area Example</TITLE></HEAD>
<BODY>
<MAP NAME="istanbulmap">
  <AREA COORDS="43,129,249,158" HREF="hst.htm"
  →onMouseOver="theForm.out.value='Learn about
  →Istanbul\'s history'">
  <AREA COORDS="298,129,507,158" HREF=
  →"where.htm" onMouseOver="theForm.out.value=
  →'Make reservations.'">
  <AREA COORDS="68,201,248,230" HREF="eat.htm"
  →onMouseOver="theForm.out.value='Reviews of
  →hundreds of restaurants.'">
  <AREA COORDS="299,201,531,230" HREF=
  →"transport.htm" onMouseOver="theForm.out
  →.value='Travel by bus, train, or taxi.'">
  <AREA COORDS="276,323,51" HREF="turkey.htm"
  →SHAPE="circle" onMouseOver="theForm.out
  →.value='Go to the Turkey home page.'">
</MAP><CENTER>
<IMG SRC="istanbul.gif" BORDER=0 USEMAP=
→"#istanbulmap">
<FORM NAME="theForm">
<INPUT TYPE="text" NAME="out" SIZE=40>
</FORM></CENTER></BODY></HTML>
```

Figure 8.9 This script displays a message when the user moves over an area.

Script 8.10 JavaScript can display information when the user clicks on part of an image map.

```
script
<HTML><HEAD><TITLE>Map Example</TITLE>
<SCRIPT LANGUAGE="JavaScript">
<!--HIDE
function detail (which) {
    document.images[0].src = which + ".gif"
}
//STOP HIDING-->
</SCRIPT></HEAD>
<BODY>
<IMG SRC="intro.gif">
<BR><H3>Click on an area to see detail:</H3>
<MAP NAME="imap">
    <AREA COORDS="126,0,379,124" HREF=
    →"javascript:detail('i1')">
    <AREA COORDS="135,153,387,277" HREF=
    →"javascript:detail('i2')">
    <AREA COORDS="0,25,124,277" HREF=
    →"javascript:detail('i3')">
</MAP>
<IMG SRC="minimap.gif" USEMAP="#imap">
</BODY></HTML>
```

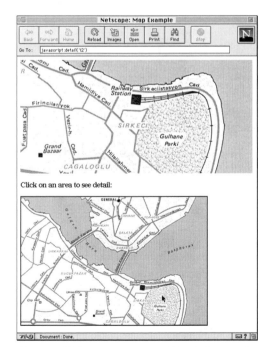

Figure 8.10 An interactive map of Istanbul shows the user details of the part she clicks on.

MAKING AN INTERACTIVE MAP

You generally use image maps to link to different pages. You can use JavaScript, however, to display the information on the same page, making your site faster and easier to use.

Script 8.10, for example, displays a detail of the area the user selects. Because areas cannot use **onClick**, the script uses a JavaScript link instead.

To create an interactive image map:

1. function detail(which) {

Define a function with one argument, a reference to the new image (see page 38).

2. document.images[0].src = which + ".gif" }

Use the equals sign to assign the name of your argument followed by **+** "**.gif**" to your image source (see page 23).

2. <AREA COORDS="135,153,387,277" HREF="javascript:detail('i2')">

<AREA COORDS="135,153,387,277"
                            >

Use **<AREA>** and specify its coordinates to define a link within your HTML map.

HREF=

Type **HREF=** to assign the area's link.

"javascript:detail   "

Within quotation marks, type **javascript** in all lowercase followed by a colon and the name of your function. Page 42 explains JavaScript links.

('i2')

Pass your function the file name of the information to display. Script 8.10 displays a more detailed image.

3. <IMG SRC="minimap.gif" USEMAP="#imap">

Define an HTML image tag and specify the name of your map in its usemap attribute (see page 120).

CHANGING THE LINKS OF A MAP

You can use one HTML map tag to offer multiple maps to the user by changing its links and images. See Figure 8.11.

To change the links of an image map:

1. for (var i = 0; i < 5; i++) {

Within a function, create a for loop to cycle through each of the map's links. See page 74 for an explanation of for loops.

2. document.links[i].href = "adana" + i

document.links[i]

Within this loop, address the appropriate link by using your counter as its index number (see page 77).

OR document.hst

You can also address the area by name.

.href =

Type the name of a link property (see Table 7.3 on page 106).

"adana" + i

Assign the destination URL. Its name should include your counter variable.

3. document.images[0].src="Adana.gif"

document.images[0].src

After the loop, address the source of your map's image (see page 116).

=

Type the equals sign.

"Adana.gif"

Type the name of the new map image within quotation marks to tell JavaScript to put it in place of the original.

CHANGING THE LINKS OF AN IMAGE MAP

Script 8.11 You can change a map's image source and links.

```
<HTML><HEAD><TITLE>Map and Links</TITLE>
<SCRIPT LANGUAGE="JavaScript">
<!--HIDE
function changeIt() {
    for (var i = 0; i < 5; i++) {
        document.links[i].href = "adana" + i
    }
    document.images[0].src="Adana.gif"
}
//STOP HIDING-->
</SCRIPT></HEAD>
<BODY>
<MAP NAME="cityMap">
    <AREA COORDS="43,129,249,158" NAME="hst"
    →HREF="hst.htm">
    <AREA COORDS="298,129,507,158" NAME="where"
    →HREF="where.htm">
    <AREA COORDS="68,201,248,230" NAME="eat"
    →HREF="eat.htm">
    <AREA COORDS="299,201,531,230" NAME="trans"
    →HREF="transport.htm">
    <AREA COORDS="276,323,51" NAME="turkey"
    →HREF="turkey.htm">
</MAP>
<IMG SRC="istanbul.gif" BORDER=0 USEMAP=
→"#cityMap">
<FORM><INPUT TYPE="button" VALUE="Next City"
→onClick="changeIt()"
</FORM></BODY></HTML>
```

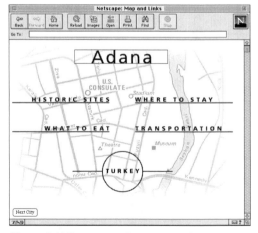

Figure 8.11 You can use the same coordinate map over another image with new links.

DATES AND ARRAYS

In Chapter 6 you saw that JavaScript makes it easy to work with simple information: text, numbers, and Booleans. But sometimes you'll want to work with more complex kinds of information. The Date and Array objects enable your scripts to handle dates and groups of variables.

You use **Date** to work with times and dates in your scripts. You can store a particular time and manipulate its parts.

You saw on page 29 how JavaScript uses arrays to access and store information about your document, such as the forms and images it contains. JavaScript also lets you create your own arrays to group together sets of related information, such as the words in a string. In this chapter we'll show you how to work with these groupings.

DISPLAYING THE CURRENT DATE

Computers keep track of the current time with an internal clock. You can store the time by creating a new date variable. Whenever you want to store a date, you use the Date constructor to create an instance, as described on page 34.

To display the current date:

1. var today = new Date()

> **var today =**
>
> Within your script, create a variable and use the equals sign to assign it your new date.

> **new**
>
> Type **new** to tell JavaScript that you want to make a new instance (see page 34).

> **Date()**
>
> Specify that you want to use the Date constructor and follow its name with parentheses. As you'll see on page 126, if you put information in the parentheses you can store dates other than the present.

2. alert("The current date is: " + today)

> Insert a message and the name of your Date variable within the parentheses of an **alert()**. As in Figure 9.1, JavaScript displays the current time in the form **Fri Dec 31 23:59:59 1999**. Although JavaScript stores other information, such as the user's time zone, it does not display it.

Script 9.1 You can store the current date and time according to the user's machine.

```
<HTML>
<HEAD><TITLE>client-side date example</TITLE>
<SCRIPT LANGUAGE="JavaScript">
<!--HIDE
function timer() {
  var today = new Date()
  alert("The current date is: " + today)
}
//STOP HIDING-->
</SCRIPT></HEAD>
<BODY><FORM>
<INPUT TYPE="button" VALUE="Check the Time"
→onClick="timer()">
</FORM></BODY></HTML>
```

Figure 9.1 JavaScipt displays dates in this form (Day Month Date hh:mm:ss yyyy).

Table 9.1

Date object	
METHODS (GET-)	
getDate()	returns an integer from 1 – 31
getDay()	returns 0 (Sunday) – 6 (Saturday)
getHours()	returns 0 (midnight) – 23 (11 pm)
getMinutes()	returns 0 – 59
getMonth()	returns 0 (January) – 11 (December)
getSeconds()	returns 0 – 59
getTime()	returns number of milliseconds since Jan 1, 1970
getTimezoneOffset()	returns difference between Greenwich Mean Time and local time in minutes
getYear()	returns last two digits of the year

Script 9.2 JavaScript allows you to isolate the components of a stored date.

```
<HTML><HEAD>
<TITLE>Making a Time-Specific Page</TITLE>
<SCRIPT LANGUAGE="JavaScript">
<!--HIDE
var time = new Date()
var hours = time.getHours()
function decide() {
  if (hours > 22 || hours < 6) {
    document.write("<IMG SRC='moon.gif'>
    →<H2>Go to bed, you raving bug-eyed
    →insomniac!</H2>")
  }
}
//STOP HIDING-->
</SCRIPT></HEAD><BODY onLoad="decide()">
</BODY></HTML>
```

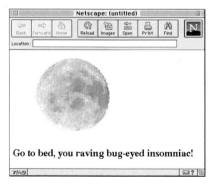

Figure 9.2 By testing the current hour, you can create a time-specific page.

WORKING WITH PART OF A DATE

You don't always need all of the information in a date. To work with a part of the date, such as the hour or day, you use the appropriate get- method, all of which are listed in Table 9.1.

You might find that the values these methods return are a little unexpected. For example, if the current month is January, **getMonth()** will return 0 instead of 1. There's no good reason for this, other than the fact that JavaScript likes to count from zero.

One way you might put use these methods to customize the content of a page based on the time the user accesses it. Script 9.2, for example, tests the hour on the user's machine and alters its greeting accordingly.

To work with part of a date:

1. var time = new Date()

Store the current date and time.

2. var hours = time.getHours()

> time

Type the name of your date variable.

> .getHours()

Type a dot followed by **get** and the part of the date you want (see Table 9.1). **GetHours()** returns an integer from 0 to 23.

var hours =

Create a variable and use the equals sign to store the part of the date you have chosen.

STORING A SPECIFIC DATE

Sometimes you need to store a time other than the present. Script 9.3, for example, stores the day that it was created so that it can determine how long it has been in existence when the user visits.

To store a date, you need to specify it in a format that JavaScript can understand. There are two such formats: a list of numbers separated by commas (99, 12, 31, 23, 59, 59) and a string (December 31, 1999 23:59:59). You should not work with dates before January 1, 1970.

To store a specific date:

var fixed = new Date(97, 03, 04, 09, 30, 22)

1. var fixed =

Create a new variable and use the equals sign to store your new date.

2. new

Type **new** to tell JavaScript that you are creating a new object (see page 34).

3. Date( )

Specify the Date constructor.

4. 97, 03, 04, 09, 30, 22

Type the year, month, day, hour, minute and second that you wish to store separated by commas. You can leave off the hour, minute, and second to set them to zero.

OR "March 04, 1997 09:30:22"

You can also write out the date you want surrounded by quotation marks. You can leave off the time, but you must write out the complete name of the month (i.e., January not Jan).

Script 9.3 You can specify a date other than present for JavaScript to store.

```
script
<HTML>
<HEAD><TITLE>Creating a set date</TITLE>
<SCRIPT LANGUAGE="JavaScript">
<!--HIDE
function compare() {
   var fresh=new Date()
   var fixed=new Date(97,03,04,09,30,22)
   var enterdate=new Date(document.forms[0]
   →.elements[0].value)
   monthOne=fresh.getMonth()
   monthTwo=fixed.getMonth()
   alert("You\'re visiting this page " +
   →(monthOne-monthTwo) + " months after its
   →inception.")
}
//STOP HIDING-->
</SCRIPT></HEAD>
<BODY><FORM>
<INPUT TYPE="text" onChange="compare()">
</FORM></BODY></HTML>
```

Figure 9.3 This script subtracts a month defined in the script from the current month to determine how long ago the script was written.

Table 9.2

Date object	
METHODS (SET-)	
setDate(n)	sets the date to n
setHours(n)	sets the hours to n
setMinutes(n)	sets the minutes to n
setMonth(n)	sets the day of the month to n
setSeconds(n)	sets the seconds to n
setTime(n)	sets the number of milliseconds since 1/1/70 to n
setYear(n)	sets the day of the month to n

Script 9.4 The getDate method retrieves the date of a Date object, and setDate() alters its value.

```
<HTML><HEAD><TITLE>Date Setting Example</TITLE>
<SCRIPT LANGUAGE="JavaScript">
<!--HIDE
var when = new Date()
function moneyDue() {
  when.setDate(when.getDate() + 30)
  alert("You need not pay a penny for these
→goods until " + (when.getMonth()+1) + "."+
→when.getDate() + "." + when.getYear())
}
//STOP HIDING-->
</SCRIPT></HEAD>
<BODY><FORM>
<INPUT TYPE="button" VALUE="Buy our Product"
→onClick="moneyDue()">
</FORM></BODY>
</HTML>
```

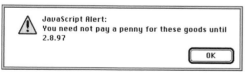

JavaScript Alert:
You need not pay a penny for these goods until
2.8.97

OK

Figure 9.4 This script determines the date thirty days from the current day.

CHANGING PART OF A DATE

Once you've stored a date you can change a single part it. You do this with the **set-** methods, which are listed in Table 9.2.

JavaScript is pretty smart when it comes to altering dates. For example, if you change the month, it changes the day of the week accordingly.

You can the **set-** methods in combination with the **get-** methods (see page 125) to set a date relative to the present.

To change part of a date:

1. var when = new Date()

Create a new variable and store the current date.

2. when.setDate(when.getDate() + 30)

when

Type the name of your date variable.

   .setDate(   )

Type a dot followed by **set** and the part of the date you want to change.

   when.getDate()

Use the appropriate **get-** method to determine the current value of the part of the date you want to change.

   + 30

Add the desired quantity to the current value to advance it. Script 9.4 calculates a day thirty days from the present. If you set the date to a number greater than 31 JavaScript changes the month for you.

CONVERTING TO THE USER'S TIME

When you store a date in JavaScript, it is automatically in the user's local time. Because of this, you will often need to convert between time zones. The Date object includes two methods for accomplishing this.

ToGMTString() converts a date to Greenwich Mean Time (the time in Greenwich, England, a world standard) and gives it to you as a string for display. For example, if the user is on the East Coast and your date variable stores Fri Mar 21 22:00:00 1997, toGMTString() will return Sat, 22 Mar 1997 03:00:00 GMT.

To perform more general conversions, you can use **getTimezoneOffset()**, which returns the time difference, in minutes, between the user's local time and GMT. With this information you can easily adjust fixed times for the user's time zone.

To convert to the user's time zone:

1. var when = new Date(97,3,16,10)

Create a new date and store the desired time in your local time zone.

2. var user=(when.getTimezoneOffset() / 60)

Type the name of your date variable followed by **.getTimezoneOffset()** to determine the number of minutes that the user's time differs from GMT. Divide this by sixty to convert to hours.

3. when.setHours(when.getHours() +(8 - user))

when.getHours() +(8 - user)

To determine the time difference between you and the user, subtract the user's offset from GMT from the offset of your local time zone. Add this to the hour you stored in your date variable (see page 126). This converts to the user's local time.

when.setHours(   )

Change the stored hour to the new time.

Script 9.5 GetTimezoneOffset() allows for time difference conversions.

```
<HTML><HEAD><TITLE>Converting Time Zone</TITLE>
<SCRIPT LANGUAGE="JavaScript">
<!--HIDE
var when = new Date(97,3,16,10)
var user = (when.getTimezoneOffset() / 60)
when.setHours(when.getHours() + (8 - user))
function to12h() {
   var myTime = when.getHours()
   if (when.getHours() > 12) {
      myTime -= 12
      myTime += " pm"
   }
   return myTime
}
//STOP HIDING-->
</SCRIPT></HEAD>
<BODY><CENTER>
<H1>California Media Corp.</H1><HR>
<H3>The World Power Corp. Surfing Competition
will be broadcast live from Venice Beach on
April 16 at 10 am Pacific Time.<BR><BR>
<SCRIPT LANGUAGE="JavaScript">
<!--HIDE
document.write("It will be shown in your
→time zone at " + to12h() +".")
//STOP HIDING-->
</SCRIPT></BODY></HTML>
```

Figure 9.5 This script converts a date in your time zone to the user's local time.

Script 9.6 Using the get- methods of the Date object you can create an updating clock.

```
script

<HTML>
<HEAD><TITLE>Clock Example</TITLE>
<SCRIPT LANGUAGE="JavaScript">
<!--HIDE
function showTime() {
  var now = new Date()
  var hrs = now.getHours()
  var disp = ((hrs>12) ? (hrs-12) : hrs) + ":"
  disp += now.getMinutes() + ":" +
  →now.getSeconds()
  disp += ((hrs > 12) ? " PM" : "AM")
  status = disp
  setTimeout("showTime()",1000)
}
//STOP HIDING-->
</SCRIPT></HEAD>
<BODY onLoad="showTime()">
</BODY></HTML>
```

```
ᴊ/⟲)  3:38:16 PM                    ✉ ? ▣
```

Figure 9.6 This script updates the time each second.

CREATING A CLOCK

Many sites use JavaScript to create an updating clock. You can use the **get-** methods (see page 125) to display the current time in the status bar (as we've done in Script 9.6), a text field, or even graphically on the page.

To create a clock:

1. function showTime() {

   Define a function that will display the current time.

2. var now = new Date()

   At the start of the function, store the current time in a variable (see page 124).

3. var hrs = now.getHours()

   Store the current hour using **getHours()**.

4. var disp+=((hrs > 12) ? (hrs - 12) : hrs) + ":"

   var disp

   Create a new variable in which you will store the formatted time for display.

   +=((hrs > 12) ? (hrs - 12) : hrs) + ":"

   Use **+=** to add the current hour followed by a colon to your display variable. To display the time in 12-hour format, you can use a conditional expression (see page 72) which subtracts twelve from the current hour.

5. disp += now.getMinutes() + ":" + now.getSeconds()

   Use **+=** to add the current minutes and seconds to your display variable.

6. status = disp

   Type **status** followed by **=** and the name of your display variable to update the current time in the status bar (see page 101).

7. setTimeout("showTime()", 1000)

   As the function's last line, use **setTimeout** to trigger your function after a pause (see page 102). You should specify a delay of **1000** to update the clock each second.

GENERATING A RANDOM NUMBER

If you're creating a page that uses a random number, and want it to work with versions before Navigator 3.0, you'll need to avoid the random method (see page 91). Instead you can use the function **randy** in Script 9.7. It's okay if you don't understand how it works, you can just copy the entire function into your script.

Randy generates a random number based on the current time. To do this, it uses **getTime()**, which returns the number of milliseconds since January 1, 1970 rounded to nearest second. This provides a large number that varies each second. **Randy** manipulates this number to ensure that it is an integer within the chosen range of values.

To generate a random number:

1. Copy the entire function **randy** from Script 9.7 into your script. You should put it in the head portion of your HTML document.

2. randy(this.form.low, this.form.high)

randy(   )

Within your script, wherever you want to insert a random number, type **randy** followed by parentheses.

this.form.low

Type the lowest possible number that you want returned. Script 9.7 allows the user to enter this number in a text field.

, this.form.high

Type a comma followed by the largest number you want to be returned. Script 9.7 reads this number from a text field.

Script 9.7 You can use this function to generate random numbers for Navigator 2.0.

```
                          script

<HTML><HEAD><TITLE>Random Generator</TITLE>
<SCRIPT LANGUAGE="JavaScript">
<!--HIDE
function randy(loField,hiField) {
    var lo = parseInt(loField.value)
    var hi = parseInt(hiField.value) - 1
    var now = new Date()
    var rnd = 98726471 * (now.getTime() /
    →((now.getMinutes() + 1) * 1000))
    rnd = lo + Math.floor(rnd % (hi - lo))
    return rnd
}
//STOP HIDING-->
</SCRIPT></HEAD>
<BODY><FORM>
<H2>Give me a random integer between <INPUT
TYPE="text" NAME="low" SIZE=3> and <INPUT
TYPE="text" NAME="high" SIZE=3>:<BR>
<INPUT TYPE="text" NAME="tellme" SIZE=3>
<INPUT TYPE="button" VALUE="random"
→onClick="this.form.tellme.value =
→randy(this.form.low,this.form.high)">
</FORM></BODY></HTML>
```

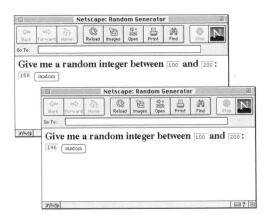

Figure 9.7 The user enters the range of possible random numbers.

Script 9.8 You can fill an array at the time of creation or later by assignment.

```
script
<HTML><HEAD><TITLE>Creating an Array</TITLE>
<SCRIPT LANGUAGE="JavaScript">
<!--HIDE
var change = 0
function dense() {
  var colors = new Array("tan","peru","wheat")
  document.bgColor=colors[change]
  if (change < 2) {
    change += 1
    setTimeout("dense()", 1000)
  }
}
function explicit() {
  var colors = new Array(3)
  var myColor = document.forms[0].elements
  →[change].value
  colors[change] = myColor
  document.bgColor = colors[change]
  if (change < 2) {
    change += 1
    setTimeout("explicit()", 1000)
  }
}
//STOP HIDING--></SCRIPT></HEAD>
<BODY><FORM><H2>
Color 1:<INPUT TYPE="text"><BR>
Color 2:<INPUT TYPE="text"><BR>
Color 3:<INPUT TYPE="text"> <BR>
<INPUT TYPE="button" VALUE="Earth Tones"
→onClick="dense()">
<INPUT TYPE="button" VALUE="My Colors"
→onClick="explicit()">
</H2></FORM></BODY></HTML>
```

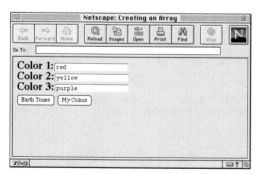

Figure 9.8 One button triggers the use of a pre-filled array. The other reads the text field values into array entries.

CREATING AN ARRAY

Like the arrays you have used in the JavaScript hierarchy, arrays you create store related pieces of information. You can put any type of information into an array entry: a number, Boolean, or string. You can then refer to your entries by number starting at zero for the first entry.

You create arrays with Navigator 3.0's Array constructor (see page 34). You can tell JavaScript what to put in the array entries or how many entries there should be.

To create an array:

1. var colors = new Array(3)

var colors =

Create a variable to store your new array.

new

Type **new** to tell JavaScript that you want to create an object (see page 34).

Array( )

Specify the Array constructor to make a set of indexed entries.

3

Type the number of entries you want your new array to contain. Each of these will store **null** until you assign it a value.

OR   "tan","peru", "wheat"

Type the values you want your array to contain. JavaScript puts these in your array's entries starting with entry zero.

2. colors[0] = myColor

To fill a particular entry, type the name of your array and the entry's number in brackets. Use the equals sign to assign it a value.

CREATING AN ARRAY

If you want your script to run on Navigator 2.0, you'll need an alternative way to make arrays. As you saw on page 34, you can use a constructor called **Object** to create an empty object.

You can give your object properties by name or by number. If you assign them by number, your object will work in almost exactly the same way as an array.

To create an array in Navigator 2.0:

1. var imgs = new Object()

> var imgs =

Within your script, create a variable to store your array.

> new

Type **new** to create a new object.

> Object()

Specify the Object constructor and add parentheses. This creates an object with no properties or methods (see page 34).

2. imgs[0] = "pen.gif"

> imgs[0]

To fill an entry, type the name of your variable followed by the number of the desired entry in brackets (see page 30).

> = "pen.gif"

Use the equals sign to assign your chosen entry a value. Script 9.9 assigns image sources to its array entries.

3. document.write("<IMG SRC='" + imgs[pick] + "'>")

To access an entry, type the name of your variable followed by the number of the desired entry in brackets.

Script 9.9 You can use an empty object to substitute for an array in Navigator 2.0.

```
<HTML>
<HEAD><TITLE>Array Example</TITLE></HEAD>
<BODY><CENTER>
<SCRIPT LANGUAGE="JavaScript">
<!--HIDE
var imgs = new Object()
imgs[0] = "pen.gif"
imgs[1] = "money.gif"
imgs[2] = "lamp.gif"
imgs[3] = "folks.gif"
function randy(lo,hi) {
    hi -= 1
    var now = new Date()
    var rnd = 98726471 * (now.getTime() /
    →((now.getMinutes() + 1) * 1000))
    rnd = lo + Math.floor(rnd % (hi - lo))
    return rnd
}
function pick() {
    var pick = randy(0,4)
    document.write("<IMG SRC='" + imgs[pick]
    → + "'>")
}
pick()
//STOP HIDING-->
</SCRIPT></CENTER></BODY></HTML>
```

Figure 9.9 This script uses an array of image source names to select a random image.

Table 9.3

Array object

METHODS

join("")	joins array elements into a string separated by commas. If you give it a separator, it uses this instead.
reverse()	reverses order of entries
sort(function)	sorts array elements in alphabetical order. If you give it a comparison function, this order is used instead.

Script 9.10 You can use reverse() to flip the order of an array's entries.

```
<HTML>
<HEAD><TITLE>Reverse example</TITLE>
<SCRIPT LANGUAGE="JavaScript">
<!--HIDE
function revem() {
  var opts = new Array()
  for (var i = 0; i < 3; i++) {
    opts[i] = document.forms[0].elements[0]
    →.options[i].text
  }
  opts.reverse()
  for (var i = 0; i < 3; i++) {
    document.forms[0].elements[0].options[i]
    →.text = opts[i]
  }
}
//STOP HIDING-->
</SCRIPT></HEAD>
<BODY><FORM><SELECT>
<OPTION>Item 1
<OPTION>Item 2
<OPTION>Item 3
</SELECT>
<INPUT TYPE="button" VALUE="reverse"
→onClick="rev()">
</FORM></BODY></HTML>
```

REVERSING AN ARRAY

One advantage to using an array is that you can change how its information is ordered. Table 9.3 lists the three techniques for doing this and the next three pages discuss them.

Once you have stored information in an array, you can reverse the order of the entries. Script 9.10, for example, reorders the items in a select menu. You do this with the reverse method.

To reverse the order of array entries:

1. var opts = new Array()

   Create an array and store the desired values in it (see page 131).

2. opts.reverse()

   opts

   Type the name of your array variable to address it.

   .reverse()

   Type a dot followed by **reverse** and parentheses to tell JavaScript to reverse the order of the array's entries (see Figure 9.10).

Figure 9.10 When the user clicks the reverse button, the script reverses the order of the options.

JOINING ARRAY ENTRIES

Once you have put information into an array you may need to display it. Because each entry is separate, you will need combine them first. You can do this with the join method.

Join() normally makes your entries into one long string with commas between each entry. You can also give it an alternative string with which it will separate the values.

To join array entries:

1. var letters = new Array()

Within your script, create an array and store the desired values in it (see page 131).

2. var str2 = letters.join("")

var str2 =

Create a new variable to store the joined entries.

letters

Type the name of your array variable.

.join( )

Type a dot followed by join to tell JavaScript to put all of the entries into a single string.

""

Type the desired separator in quotation marks. You can use a null string ("") to join the entries without separation, as in Script 9.11. If you do not specify a separator, JavaScript uses a comma.

Figure 9.11 This script stores the user's text in an array of characters, reverses them, and then joins them to determine if the text is a palindrome.

Script 9.11 You can use join() to put all of the entries into a single string.

```
<HTML><HEAD><TITLE>Join and Reverse</TITLE>
<SCRIPT LANGUAGE="JavaScript">
<!--HIDE
function flipper(theField) {
   var str=theField.value
   var letters=new Array()
   for (var i=0;i<str.length;i++) {
      letters[i]=str.charAt(i)
   }
   letters.reverse()
   var str2 = letters.join("")
   if (str2 == str) {
      alert("Oh! You made a palindrome.")
   }
}
//STOP HIDING-->
</SCRIPT>
<BODY><FORM>
<H2><CENTER>The Astounding Palindrome Tester
</H2></CENTER>
<INPUT TYPE="text" SIZE=25
→onChange="flipper(this)">
</FORM></BODY></HTML>
```

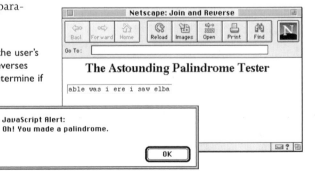

JOINING ARRAY ENTRIES

Script 9.12 Sort() reorders the entries in an array alphabetically.

```
                    script
<HTML><HEAD><TITLE>Sort Example</TITLE>
<SCRIPT LANGUAGE="JavaScript">
<!--HIDE
function orderIt(theField) {
   var chaos = theField.value
   var order = chaos.split(" ")
   order.sort()
   theField.value = order.join(" ")
}
//STOP HIDING-->
</SCRIPT></HEAD>
<BODY><FORM>
<H2>Enter words to alphabetize:</H2>
<TEXTAREA ROWS=4 COLS=40 WRAP="virtual">
</TEXTAREA>
<INPUT TYPE="button" VALUE="alphabetize"
→onClick="orderIt(this.form.elements[0])">
</FORM></BODY></HTML>
```

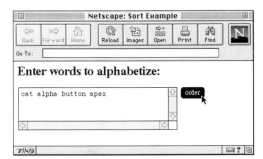

Figure 9.12 This script uses the sort method to alphabetize the user's text.

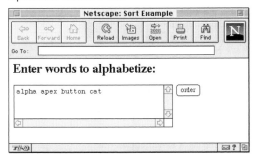

SORTING ENTRIES ALPHABETICALLY

If you have an array of entries that you want to alphabetize, JavaScript can do it for you.

Sort() compares your entries on a character-by-character basis. The first unequal character determines the order of the sort. No matter what types of information you give it, **sort()** treats everything as a string. Because of this, you'll find that numbers are not correctly ordered. For example, it will place the value **82** before the value **9**. You can sort numbers with the technique discussed on the next page.

To sort entries alphabetically:

1. var order = chaos.split(" ")

Within your script, create an unordered array of strings. You can use **split()** to divide text entered by the user into an array (see page 89). Script 9.12 splits at spaces to divide the entries by word.

2. order.sort()

order

Type the name of your array variable.

.sort()

Type a dot followed by **sort** and parentheses to tell JavaScript you want to sort using alphabetical order. As you'll see on the next page, you can specify a function within the parentheses to use a different order.

SORTING ENTRIES NUMERICALLY

Alphabetical order isn't appropriate for all types of information. If you want to sort a set of numbers, for example, you'll need to use different criteria. In situations like this, you can give JavaScript a function that tells it how to compare values, as in Script 9.13.

This function, called a comparison function, always uses two arguments. As it sorts, JavaScript gives your function two values at a time to figure out what order they should be in. You signal the correct order with the number your function returns.

To Sort entries numerically:

1. function compare (a, b) {

function compare (   ) {

Define a function which JavaScript will use to determine the correct order of your entries.

a, b

Within the parentheses, specify the names of two arguments. JavaScript uses these to give your function two values to compare.

2. return (a - b) }

As the last line of your function, type **return** followed by **a - b** in parentheses. Because you're comparing numbers, you can subtract the second from the first to determine the correct order. If **a** is greater than **b**, a positive result signals that **b** should be first. If **b** is greater, a negative result signals that the original order should be maintained.

3. order.sort(compare)

Within your script, address sort and type the name of your comparison function in parentheses.

Script 9.13 JavaScript lets you specify any ordering criteria in a function.

```
<HTML><HEAD><TITLE>Sorting Numbers</TITLE>
<SCRIPT LANGUAGE="JavaScript">
<!--HIDE
function compare (a,b) {
   return a - b
}
function orderIt(theField) {
   var chaos = theField.value
   var order = chaos.split(" ")
   order.sort(compare)
   theField.value = order.join("")
}
//STOP HIDING-->
</SCRIPT></HEAD>
<BODY><FORM>
<H2>Enter numbers to order:</H2>
<TEXTAREA ROWS=10 COLS=40 "></TEXTAREA>
<INPUT TYPE="button" VALUE="order"
→onClick="orderIt(this.form.elements[0])">
</FORM></BODY></HTML>
```

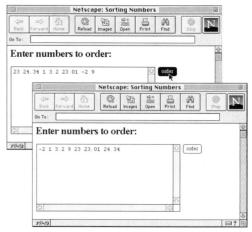

Figure 9.13 You can use a comparison function to sort user input in numerical order.

FRAMES AND WINDOWS

10

Table 10.1

window object (multiple windows)	
PROPERTIES	**METHODS**
self the current window	focus() brings to front
name used to address window	blur() sends to back
opener calling window	open() opens new window
EVENT HANDLERS	close() closes window
onFocus user enters window	
onBlur user leaves window	

JavaScript allows you to create frames and windows that interact with one another. You can open and close new windows and pass information between windows and frames.

In this chapter we will show you how to use these techniques to create more user-friendly sites.

JavaScript works with windows by using the window object. It also uses a frames object, but JavaScript generally thinks of each frame as a subwindow of the complete browser window. Table 10.1 lists the properties, methods, and event handlers of **window**.

OPENING A NEW WINDOW

..NING A NEW WINDOW

You can open new windows with your script using **open()**, as in Script 10.1. This allows you to control the window's content and features (size, scrollbar, and so on). The only thing you can't control is the new window's location on the screen.

To open a new window:

var myWin = window.open("beauty.html", "picture" ,"status=no,width=300,height=200")

1. var myWin =

Declare a variable. You will use it to store a reference to the new window.

2. open(
)

Type **open()** to tell JavaScript that you want to open a new window.

3. "beauty.html"

Within quotation marks, type the location of the HTML file for the new window.

4. ,"picture"

After a comma, specify a name for the new window. You will use this name if you target the new window with links on other pages.

5. ,"status=no, "

After a comma, specify the features for your new window in quotation marks. Type = **no** after the name of a window feature you don't want or = **yes** after one you do. Figure 10.2 illustrates all of the features you can set. If you don't specify any features, they will all default to **yes**. If you set at least one of them to **no**, as in Script 10.1, you must set the ones you want to **yes**. Separate your feature assignments with commas.

6. width=300,height=200

Within the quotation marks, specify the window's width and height in pixels.

Script 10.1 You can open new windows from within your scripts.

```
<HTML><HEAD><TITLE>new window</TITLE>
<SCRIPT LANGUAGE="JavaScript">
<!--HIDE
function openArt() {
    var myWin = window.open("beauty.html",
    →"picture","status=no,width=300,height=200")
}
//STOP HIDING-->
</SCRIPT></HEAD>
<BODY NAME="main"><CENTER>
<H1>The Great Art Page!</H1>
<A HREF="#" onClick="openArt()">
<IMG SRC="show.gif"></A>
</CENTER></BODY></HTML>
```

Figure 10.1 You can control the size, contents, and features of the second window.

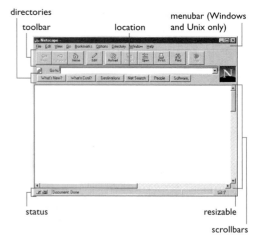

Figure 10.2 When opening a window, you can choose which features to display.

Script 10.2 If you open a window in your script, you can close both the new one and the original.

```
                        script
<HTML><HEAD>
<TITLE>beauty.html</TITLE></HEAD>
<BODY><CENTER>
<IMG SRC="art.gif" WIDTH=250><BR>
<FORM>
<INPUT TYPE="button" VALUE="CLOSE THIS →WIN-
DOW" onClick="self.close()">
<INPUT TYPE="button" VALUE="CLOSE THE →OTHER
WINDOW" onClick="opener.close()">
</FORM></CENTER></BODY></HTML>
```

Figure 10.3 When the user clicks a link in one window, this script opens a new one. If the user tries to close the original from the new window, JavaScript asks for confirmation.

CLOSING A WINDOW

In Navigator 2.0, a script could close any window without warning. Navigator 3.0 limits this ability because so many people abused it. You can close any window, but if JavaScript didn't open it, it will confirm the close with the user (see Figure 10.3).

If your page has opened a second window, you can close it with the variable name you used when you opened it. You can use **self** to close the current window and **opener** to close the window that opened the current one.

To close a window:

onClick="self.close()"

1. self

Within the script of the window you want to close, type **self** to address this window. If you leave this out JavaScript will assume you want to close the current window, but you should use **self** to clarify your code. Script 10.3 addresses **self** from an event handler (see page 32).

OR opener

Type **opener** to address the window which opened the current one.

2. .close()

Type **.close** followed by parentheses to close the window you have addressed. If JavaScript opened this window, it will close it immediately. If JavaScript.didn't open the window, it will ask the user to confirm the close.

CREATING A NAVIGATION BAR

Many pages on the Web use a second frame as a navigation bar, a document that contains links targeting the main frame. Because they never change, navigation bars make your site more consistent.

Using JavaScript, you can open a new window and use this as a navigation bar. This has the advantage of not interfering with the main display and letting the user close the navigation bar from the main window.

To create a floating navigation bar:

1. winTwo=window.open("nav.html","Navigate", "width=175,height=470")

winTwo=window.open("nav.html",
)

Within your script, open a new window which contains the HTML document for your navigation bar.

"width=175,height=470"

Specify the window's size. You will probably want a navigation window which is clearly horizontal or vertical. Script 10.3 opens a vertical window.

2. self.name = "main"

Within the main window's script, use the equals sign to assign a name to **self.name** (see page 139).

3. <A HREF="press.html" TARGET="main">

<A HREF="press.html"   >

Within the HTML for the second window, create links to each page or anchor that you want the navigation bar to access.

                    TARGET="main"

Within the link tags, type **TARGET=** and the name you gave to the main window in quotation marks.

Script 10.3 The links in the navigation bar target the main window.

```
script
<HTML><HEAD><TITLE>main</TITLE>
<SCRIPT LANGUAGE="JavaScript">
<!--HIDE
var winTwo = null
function openNav() {
  winTwo = window.open("nav.html",
  →"Navigate","width=175,height=470")
  self.name = "main"
}
function closeNav() {
  if (winTwo != null) {
    winTwo.close()
  }
}
function exploit() {
  alert("You have just sent 30 children to
```

```
script
<HTML><HEAD><TITLE>Navigate</TITLE></HEAD>
<BODY><CENTER>
<H4>P O W E R !<HR WIDTH=50%>
<A HREF="prop.html" TARGET="main">
<IMG SRC="money.gif" BORDER=0>
<BR>Capitalist Propaganda</A><BR>
<A HREF="exploit.html" TARGET="main">
<IMG SRC="folks.gif" BORDER=0>
<BR>Exploitation of Third World
Nations</A><BR>
<A HREF="press.html" TARGET="main">
<IMG SRC="pen.gif" BORDER=0>
<BR>Press Releases</A><BR></H4><FORM>
<INPUT TYPE="button" VALUE="Exploit"
→onClick="opener.exploit()">
</FORM></CENTER></BODY></HTML>
```

Figure 10.4 A floating navigation bar stays the same while the main window loads new pages.

Script 10.4 After opening a floating navigation bar blur() returns the user to the main window.

```
<HTML>
<HEAD><TITLE>main</TITLE>
<SCRIPT LANGUAGE="JavaScript">
<!--HIDE
var winTwo = null
function openNav() {
   winTwo = window.open("nav.html",
   →"Navigate","width=175,height=470")
   self.name = "main"
   winTwo.blur()
}
function closeNav() {
   if (winTwo != null) {
      winTwo.close()
   }
}
//STOP HIDING-->
</SCRIPT></HEAD>
<BODY><CENTER><H1>Welcome to the World Wide
Power Corporation Home Page!</H1>
<FORM><INPUT TYPE="button" VALUE="open
→navigation window" onClick="openNav()">
<INPUT TYPE="button" VALUE="close navigation
→window" onClick="closeNav()">
</FORM></CENTER></BODY></HTML>
```

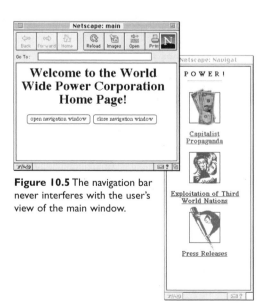

Figure 10.5 The navigation bar never interferes with the user's view of the main window.

BRINGING A WINDOW TO THE FRONT

When you open a new window with JavaScript, the first window moves to the back and the new one comes to the front. Because you can't control where the new window will appear on the screen, this can block the user's view. If your new window is a navigation bar, for example, you should return the main window to the front. With Navigator 3.0 you can control which window is in front with **focus()** and **blur()**.

Blur() sends a window to the background, as in Script 10.4 and **focus()** brings it to the foreground.

To bring a window to the front:

winTwo.blur()

1. winTwo

Within your script type the name of a variable that stores a window reference or type **self** to address the current window.

2. .blur()

Type **.blur** followed by parentheses to send the window to the background. Script 10.4 blurs a floating navigation bar after opening it.

OR .focus()

Type **.focus** followed by parentheses to bring the window to the foreground. This moves all other windows to the background.

REFERRING TO FRAMES

You use frames to display multiple pages in a single window. You can use JavaScript to make user events in one frame trigger changes in another.

To create frames in HTML, you need to use a framesetting document. Frames address this document as **parent**. In dot syntax, **parent** falls to the right of the frame name like any other property, but it points to what would normally be on the left.

A framesetting document can address its child frames by its name or its index number in **frames[ ]**. Table 10.2 lists the properties of frames.

To refer to frames:

```
onClick="parent.frames[1].frameTwoFunc()"
```

1. onClick="   "

Within the desired tag in one of your frames, type **onClick=** followed by quotation marks (see page 34).

2.   parent

Type **parent** to address the frameset that created your frame.

3.   .frames

Type **.frames** to access the frames array.

OR

.child1

You can also refer to a frame by name.

4.   [1]

Follow **frames** with brackets and the index number of a different frame. JavaScript numbers the frames in the order the framesetting document defines them.

5.   .frameTwoFunc()

Type a dot followed by the name of the variable or function you want to work with. Script 10.5 triggers a function in the second frame with a button click in the first.

Table 10.2

frame object	
PROPERTIES	
frames	frames array includes all child frames. Length is its only property.
name	value of name attribute
length	number of child frames
parent	framesetting window or frame
self	current frame
window	current frame
top	top-level frameset window

Script 10.5 It takes three HTML documents to make a window with two frames, but all three documents can address one another.

```
<HTML><TITLE>Referring to Frames</TITLE>
<FRAMESET ROWS="40%,60%">
<FRAME SRC=Frame1.html NAME="child1">
<FRAME SRC=Frame2.html NAME="child2">
</F
</H
```

```
<HTML><HEAD><TITLE>Frame 1</TITLE>
<SCRIPT LANGUAGE="JavaScript">
<!--HIDE
function frameOneFunc() {
    alert("The length of the frames array
    is" + parent.length)
    document.write("<H2>You can determine
    →the length of the frames array.</H2>")
}
//STOP HIDING--></SCRIPT></HEAD>
<BODY><FORM>
<INPUT TYPE="button" VALUE="From one
→frame..." onClick="parent.frames[1]
→.frameTwoFunc()"></FORM></BODY></HTML>
```

```
<HTML><HEAD><TITLE>Frame 2</TITLE>
<SCRIPT LANGUAGE="JavaScript">
<!--HIDE
function frameTwoFunc() {
    document.write("<BODY bgColor=
    →'papayawhip'>")
    document.write("<H2>You can call func
    →tions in another frame.</H2>")
    document.write("<FORM><INPUT TYPE='but
    →ton'VALUE='Or...'onClick='parent
    →.child1.frameOneFunc()'></FORM>")
}
//STOP HIDING-->
</SCRIPT></HEAD></HTML>
```

Script 10.6 Adding these scripts to Script 10.5 creates a nested frameset.

```
script
<HTML><TITLE>Nesting Frames</TITLE>
<FRAMESET COLS="80%,20%">
<FRAME SRC=c10-frame NAME="horizontals">
<FRAME SRC=c10-newframe NAME="vertical">
</F
</H
          script
    <HTML><BODY>
    <SCRIPT LANGUAGE="JavaScript">
    <!--HIDE
    function refer() {
      alert("My sister is: " + top.frames[0]
      →.name)
      alert("My nephew is: " + top.frames[0]
      →.frames[0].name)
      document.write("<H2>create a whole
      →hierarchy of nested frames.</H2>")
    }
    //STOP HIDING-->
    </SCRIPT>
    <FORM>
    <INPUT TYPE="button" VALUE="Or..."
    →onClick=refer()>
    </FORM></BODY></HTML>
```

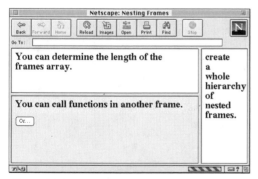

Figure 10.6 Each of these frames can trigger changes in the others.

Referring to Nested Frames

To use horizontal and vertical frames in the same window, you need to nest framesets. To create the window in Figure 10.6, for example, you need five HTML documents, the two on this page and the three listed on the previous page (see Figure 10.7).

Working with nested framesets means that you have to use a second frames array (see page 29). You can use **top** to shorten an address to the first frameset.

To refer to nested frames:

> top.frames[0].frames[0].name

1. top

> Within any of the five documents, type **top** to address the first frameset window.

2.   .frames[0]

> Type **.frames** and the index number of the nested frameset within brackets (see page 30).

3.   .frames[0]

> Type **.frames[ ]** to address this second array of frames and put the desired frame's index within the brackets.

4.   .name

> Type a dot and then the name of the property you want to access. In Script 10.6, the vertical frame alerts the name of the top horizontal frame.

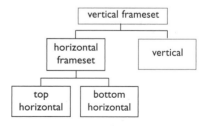

Figure 10.6 The five documents in Scripts 10.5 and 10.6 create a hierarchy of frames. The scripts on this page have a red border.

WRITING TO A WINDOW

To write from one document to another you use document.write() (see page 11). If you write over a page which has already loaded, however, this technique won't work. Instead, you need to open the document first, then write to it, and finally close it to display your changes.

Write() and writeln() automatically open the document. Until you close the document, however, only formatted text will appear (see Figure 10.8).

If you open a document, JavaScript automatically clears it. You can use clear() to erase a document without opening it.

To write to a window:

1. function fill() {

Define a function. You will use it to overwrite a document.

2. newOne.document.write("<H2>")

newOne.document

Address the document you want to overwrite. Script 10.7 changes the document of another window.

.write(   )

Type .write to open the document and write to it. Opening the document automatically clears it.

("<H2>")

Put your HTML code within parentheses.

3. onClick="newOne.document.close()"

When you are done writing to the document, address it and type .close() to display your changes. Script 10.7 triggers the closing with a button click.

4. onClick="fill()"

Put an event handler in the desired tag. Use it to trigger your function (see page 32).

Script 10.7 Once you have finished writing to a document, you must close it to display your changes.

```
<HTML><HEAD>
<TITLE>Writing to Another Window</TITLE>
<SCRIPT LANGUAGE="JavaScript">
<!--HIDE
var newOne=window.open("", "newOne",
"Width=400,height=150")
function fill() {
  newOne.document.write("<H2>")
  newOne.document.write("The data stream is
  →flowing.</H2><IMAGE SRC='happy face.gif'>")
}
//STOP HIDING-->
</SCRIPT></HEAD>
<BODY><FORM>
<INPUT TYPE="button" VALUE="finish it!"
→onClick="newOne.document.close()">
<INPUT TYPE="button" VALUE="write()"
→onClick="fill()">
</FORM></BODY></HTML>
```

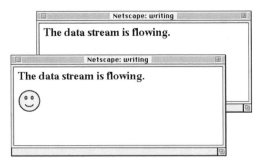

Figure 10.8 Formatted text appears before you close the document, but images do not.

Script 10.8 You can use a window or frame to store information across multiple pages.

```
script

<HTML><HEAD><TITLE>Cart</TITLE>
<SCRIPT LANGUAGE="JavaScript">
<!--HIDE
var count = 0
var purchases = new Array()
function addItem() {
  purchases[count] = opener.document
→.forms[0].prod.value
  count += 1
}
//STOP HIDING-->
</SCRIPT></HEAD>
<BODY><CENTER><A HREF="#" onClick="addItem()">
<IMG SRC="cart.gif">Add Item</A><BR><BR>
<A HREF="order.html">Check Out</A>
</CENTER></BODY></HTML>
```

Figure 10.9 This script stores the user's purchases in arrays in a shopping cart window.

STORING INFORMATION

Normally the information stored on a page disappears when the user leaves. To keep this information, you can pass it between forms with the hidden element (see page 58) or store it in a separate window.

Script 10.8 uses a "shopping cart" window, which adds the user's purchases into an array (see page 131). You can add an order form page to tally this information.

To store information across pages:

1. var count = 0

   Within the script of your shopping cart window, define a global counter variable (see page 74) which starts at zero.

2. var purchases = new Array()

   Create an array (see page 131) to store the user's purchases.

3. function addItem() {

   Define a function (see page 36) which adds items to the shopping cart window.

4. purchases[count] = opener.document. forms[0].prod.value

   purchases[count]

   Within this function, type the name of your purchases array followed by the name of your counter in brackets.

   = opener.document. forms[0].prod.value

   Use the equals sign to assign the current array entry the name of the product in the first window. This address will begin with **opener** (see page 139).

5. count +=1

   Add one to your counter variable.

6. onClick="addItem()"

   Within the desired HTML tag, trigger your function with **onClick**.

CREATING A VISUAL HISTORY BAR

You can use JavaScript to provide a visual history of the pages a user has visited.

Script 10.9 includes two of the five documents that make the page shown in Figure 10.10. The bottom frame shows the user where he has been. To use this technique, load blank images as placeholders and change them with a click on a link.

To create a visual history bar:

1. <IMAGE SRC="blank.gif">

Within the document of your history bar, create image tags and assign blank pictures to their source attributes.

2. function addImage(num, theImage) {

Within the script of your table of contents, define a function with two arguments (see page 38), the index number of the image to change and the name of its new source.

3. top.frames[1].document.images[num].src = theImage + ".gif"

top.frames[1]

Within this function, address the frame containing your history bar (see page 143).

.document.images[num].src

Address the image to add using your first argument as the index of **images[ ]**.

= theImage + ".gif"

Use = to assign the name of your second argument plus **".gif"** as the new source.

4. onClick="addImage(2,'second')"

Within link tags in the table of contents, insert **onClick** to trigger your function (see page 107). Pass it the index number of the image to be added and the name of its new source (see page 116).

Script 10.9 Clicking on links in the table of contents frame changes the image in the history frame.

```
script
<HTML><HEAD><TITLE>Table of Contents</TITLE>
<SCRIPT LANGUAGE="JavaScript">
<!--HIDE
var i=0
function addImage(num,theImage) {
    top.frames[1].document.images[num].src =
    →theImage + ".gif"
}
//STOP HIDING-->
</SCRIPT></HEAD>
<BODY>
<A HREF=main#about TARGET="main">
About Our Company</A><BR><BR><BR>
<A HREF=main#capital TARGET="main" onClick=
→"addImage(1,'first')">
Capitalist Propaganda</A><BR><BR><BR>
<A HREF=main#exploit TARGET="main" onClick=
→"addImage(2,'second')">
Exploitation of Third World Nations</A><BR><BR>
<A HREF=main#press TARGET="main" onClick=
→"addImage(3,'third')">Press Releases</A>
</
```

```
script
<HTML><HEAD><TITLE>HISTORY</TITLE></HEAD>
<BODY><IMAGE SRC="home.gif">
<IMAGE SRC="blank.gif">
<IMAGE SRC="blank.gif">
<IMAGE SRC="blank.gif">
</BODY></HTML>
```

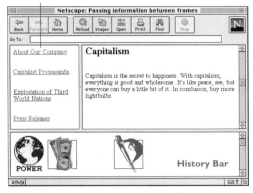

Figure 10.10 When the user clicks on a link, an icon for the new page appears in the history frame.

USER INFORMATION

To make a site successful you need to give your users a sense that it is tailored to their individual needs. Your site should know what browser the user is running and which plug-ins are installed. It should be able to access specific information about the user, such as the frequency of her visits and preferences she has set. This information lets you create a customized interface.

This chapter gives you the tools to help achieve this: the location and history objects, the navigator object, and cookies. Each of these provides a powerful means of customizing your site.

COUNTING THE NUMBER OF SITES VISITED

COUNTING THE SITES VISITED

You can use JavaScript to get information about the number of sites the user has visited and to move him to different URLs. You do these things with **location** and **history**.

The user's history is a list of the sites that he has visited in the current session, as they appear in the browser's Go menu (see Figure 11.1). You can use JavaScript to move back or forward in this list (see Table 11.2). You can also count the number of sites in the history list to determine how long the user has been browsing.

To count the number of sites the user has visited:

> window.frames[1].history.length

1. window

Within your script, type **window** or the name of a reference to another window (see page 140).

2. .frames[1]

To access a frame's history, type a dot followed by **frames** and the number of the desired frame in brackets. Each frame has its own independent history list.

3. .history

Type a dot followed by **history** to address the history object.

4. .length

Specify the length property to access the number of locations the user has visited. This is the same as the number of entries in the browser's Go menu.

Table 11.1

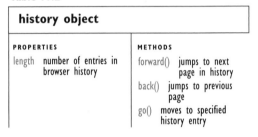

location object	
PROPERTIES	**METHODS**
hash anchor portion of URL	reload() reloads current page
host hostname and port portion of URL	replace() loads new URL over current document
hostname host and domain	
href entire URL	
pathname document's directory path	
port port number on server	
protocol beginning of URL to colon (e.g., http:)	
search query portion of URL	

Table 11.2

history object	
PROPERTIES	**METHODS**
length number of entries in browser history	forward() jumps to next page in history
	back() jumps to previous page
	go() moves to specified history entry

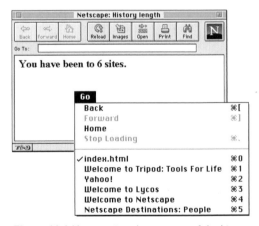

Figure 11.1 You can view the contents of the history list in the browser's Go menu and access them through the history object.

Script 11.1 Location controls the current URL.

```
<HTML>
<HEAD>
<TITLE>Changing window location</TITLE>
</HEAD>
<BODY>
<IMAGE SRC="unhappy.gif">
<FORM>
<INPUT TYPE="button" VALUE="Go Somewhere Else"
onClick="window.location = 'http://home
→.netscape.com'">
</FORM>
</BODY>
</HTML>
```

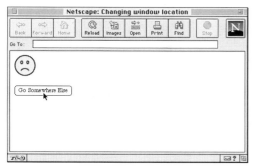

Figure 11.2 With the location object you can add a pause to a location change or trigger it with different user actions.

CHANGING THE URL OF A WINDOW

You can use JavaScript to change the user's current location. You can do this in two ways, by assigning a new URL or by moving the user back or forward in his browsing history.

You use **location** to change the current URL. It allows you to work with many parts of the address, all of which are listed in Table 11.1.

While a hypertext link provides a simple way to change location, JavaScript allows you to greater flexibility in making location changes. Script 11.1, for example, uses a button as a link. You can do this by using **location**.

To change the URL of a window:

> <INPUT TYPE="button" VALUE="Go Somewhere Else" onClick="window.location = 'http://home.netscape.com'">

1. <INPUT TYPE="button" VALUE="Go Somewhere Else" onClick="
   ">

   Insert an event handler within the desired link or button tag (see page 48).

2. window

   Type **window** to address the current window. You must include this when using **location** in an event handler.

3. .location

   Type a dot followed by **location** to access the current URL of the browser.

4. = 'http://home.netscape.com'

   Use the equals sign to specify a new location. JavaScript will make this change immediately, as if the user had clicked on a link.

MOVING TO A PRIOR URL

You can use JavaScript to move the user back or forward in the history list, as in Script 11.2. However, you'll generally only want to do this if you know a window's history, such as in a site that uses frames.

To simulate a click on the browser's Back or Forward button, you use **back()** or **forward()**. To jump to any entry in the list, you use **go()** and specify the number of entries to move.

Although you can move through the history list, JavaScript won't let you read the URLs for security reasons. If you want to find the URL of the previous page you can use **referrer** as described on page 105.

To move the window to a prior URL:

history.go(-1)

1. history

Within your script, type **history** to access the browser's history list.

2. .go(-1)

To move any number of pages back or forward, type a dot followed by **go** and the number of pages to move in parentheses. Positive numbers move forward in the list, and negative numbers move back.

OR .back()

Type a dot followed by **back** and parentheses to move to the previous URL.

OR .forward()

Type a dot followed by **forward** and parentheses to the move to the next page in the history list. If you do this when the the user has not already moved back, it will have no effect.

Script 11.2 The history methods bring the user to a prior window location.

```
script
<HTML><HEAD>
<TITLE>User History Example</TITLE>
</HEAD>
<BODY onLoad="setTimeout('history.go(-1)',
→2000)">
<IMAGE SRC="home.gif">
<H4>We're sorry to report that the World Power
Corporation is no longer in business.<BR>
Please take a moment to inform the referring
page that its link has expired.
If you came to this site directly, please
remove this address from your
bookmarks.<BR><BR>
-Thank You.</H4>
</BODY></HTML>
```

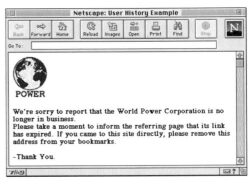

Figure 11.3 Here go() sends the user back to the previous site.

Script 11.3 Reload() triggers a reloading of the current page from the cache or server.

```
                         script

<HTML>
<HEAD><TITLE>Reload Example</TITLE>
</HEAD>
<BODY><CENTER>
<IMG SRC="/bin/gimmeone?">
<H1>WORLD POWER CORPORATION<BR>
<FORM>
<INPUT TYPE="button" VALUE="New Image"
→onClick="window.location.reload(true)">
</FORM>
</BODY>
</HTML>
```

Figure 11.4 The Check Documents setting determines whether the page is reloaded from the cache or the server.

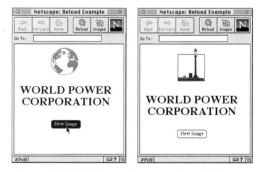

Figure 11.5 A CGI script chooses this page's image each time it loads. By triggering a reload, JavaScript causes a new image to be displayed.

RELOADING THE CURRENT PAGE

If you are working with a page that changes each time it's loaded, such as one generated by a CGI script (see Figure 11.5), you may want to trigger a reload with JavaScript, as in Script 11.3. In Navigator 3.0 you can do this with **reload()**.

There are two ways that the browser can reload a page. Either the document is read from the cache or downloaded from the server.

Normally **reload()** does exactly the same thing as clicking on the browser's Reload button. This reloads from the cache unless Check Documents Every Time is selected in the Network Preferences dialog box (see Figure 11.4) and the document has been modified.

You can also make JavaScript reload your page from the server. To do this, put **true** between the parentheses of **reload()**.

To reload the current page:

onClick="window.location.reload(true)"

1. onClick="   "

Insert an event handler within the desired HTML tag (see page 31). Script 11.3 uses **onClick** to respond to a click on a button.

2.   window.location

Address the location object (see page 149). Include **window** if you are using an event handler.

3.   .reload

Type a dot followed by reload to tell JavaScript that you want to reload the current page.

4.   (true)

Within parentheses type **true** to force the browser to reload the page from the server. Leave the parentheses empty to perform a normal reload.

REPLACING THE CURRENT PAGE

When the browser loads a new page, it normally adds the new title to the history list. To load a new page without changing the history, you can use **replace()**.

This technique prevents the user from navigating back to the original page with either the Back button or the Go menu. You may want to use page replacement when working with a page which is automatically forwarded, as in Script 11.4.

To replace the current page:

window.location.replace('http://www.ted.and .jeremy.server')

1. window

Within your script or an event handler, type **window** or the name of a variable which stores a window reference (see page 140).

2. **.location**

Type a dot followed by **location** to address the location object.

3. **.replace(**
)

Type a dot followed by **replace** and parentheses to tell JavaScript that you want to load a new page over the current one. JavaScript will not modify the history list, but the title of the original page will now refer to the new URL. This means that the user will not be able to navigate back to the replaced page.

4. **'http://www.ted.and .jeremy.server'**

Specify the URL of the replacement page within quotation marks.

Script 11.4 Replace() loads a new document over the current history entry.

```
<HTML>
<HEAD><TITLE>Replace() Example</TITLE>
<SCRIPT LANGUAGE="JavaScript">
<!--HIDE
function time() {
   setTimeout("window.location.replace('http://
   →www.ted.and.jeremy.server')", 5000)
}
//STOP HIDING-->
</SCRIPT></HEAD>
<BODY onLoad="time()">
<CENTER><H1>Attention!</H1></CENTER>
<H3>Ted and Jeremy's JavaScript site has moved
to a new URL.
Please change your bookmarks to
<H2>http://www.ted.and.jeremy.server</H2>
We'll bring you there in just a moment.
</H3></BODY></HTML>
```

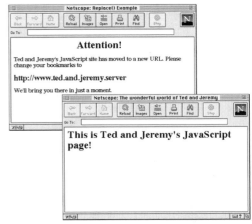

Figure 11.6 Because this script replaces the original page, the user cannot navigate back to it.

Table 11.3

navigator object	
PROPERTIES	
appName	browser type (Netscape or Microsoft Internet Explorer)
appCodeName	browser code name (Mozilla in both browsers)
appVersion	browser release number, platform, and country
userAgent	browser code name and version
mimeTypes	array of file types browser can process
plugins	array of browser's enabled plug-ins

Script 11.5 The navigator object stores information about the browser and what it can do.

```
<HTML><HEAD>
<TITLE>Using navigator example</TITLE>
<SCRIPT LANGUAGE="JavaScript">
<!--HIDE
function navShow() {
   alert("You're surfing with " + navigator
   →.appName + " "+ navigator.appCodeName +".")
}
//STOP HIDING-->
</SCRIPT></HEAD><BODY onLoad="navShow()">
</BODY></HTML>
```

Figure 11.7 You can use the navigator object to determine the user's browser.

DETERMINING THE BROWSER NAME

If you're using JavaScript features that only Navigator can handle, you should test what kind of browser the user has and only run the script if it will work.

To perform this test, you use the properties of **navigator**, as listed in Table 11.3.

To determine the browser name:

    alert(navigator.appName + navigator
    .codeName)

1.   navigator

Type **navigator** within your script to address the navigator object. You don't type anything before it because this is one of JavaScript's built-in objects (see page 27).

2.   .appName

Type **.appName**. This holds **Netscape** or **Microsoft**.

3.   navigator .codeName

Type **navigator.codeName** to access the name of the browser. This holds **Mozilla** in Navigator and **Mozilla** in Internet Explorer.

4. alert(+
)

Test these values so you can customize your script or dispay the information. Script 11.5 combines the two strings and displays them to the user.

CREATING A 3.0-SPECIFIC PAGE

Appendix B lists all of the features specific to Navigator 3.0. To determine if the user's browser can handle these, you test **userAgent**.

Running a script only on Navigator 3.0:

1. var theAgent = navigator.userAgent

var theAgent =

Within your script, define a variable to store information about the browser.

navigator.userAgent

Type **navigator.userAgent** to access a string of information about the browser. This information includes the browser code name, version number, platform, whether it is a domestic (D) or international version (I), and the processor. It is displayed in the form: **Mozilla/3.0 (Macintosh; I; PPC)**.

3. if (theAgent.indexOf("Mozilla") != -1 && theAgent.indexOf ("3.0") != -1) { setTimeout("changeImg()", 1000) }

if (&&
**   ) {**

Create a conditional to test whether the user is running Navigator and has version 3.0 (see page 67). Include your Navigator 3.0 script within the braces.

theAgent.indexOf("Mozilla") != -1

Type the name of your variable followed by **.indexOf()** (see page 88) to test whether **userAgent** contains the word "Mozilla".

!= -1

Type **!= -1** to run the statements only if the browser's code name is Mozilla (see page 68).

theAgent.indexOf ("3.0") != -1

Type the name of your variable followed by **.indexOf()** to test whether **userAgent** contains "3.0".

Script 11.6 You can test userAgent to determine if the user's browser can run your script.

```
<HTML><HEAD>
<TITLE>Determining Browser Version</TITLE>
<SCRIPT LANGUAGE="JavaScript">
<!--HIDE
var i=0
var theAgent=navigator.userAgent
if(theAgent.indexOf("Mozilla") != -1 &&
→theAgent.indexOf("3.0") != -1) {
   setTimeout("changeImg()", 1000)
}
function changeImg() {
   document.images[0].src=i + ".gif"
   i = (i < 2) ? (i + 1) : 0
   setTimeout("changeImg()", 1000)
}
//STOP HIDING-->
</SCRIPT></HEAD>
<BODY>
<IMAGE SRC="0.gif" ALIGN=left>
<BR><BR><H2> WORLDWIDE POWER CORP.</H2>
</BODY></HTML>
```

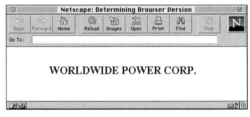

Figure 11.8 Navigator 2.0 (above) doesn't run the function that uses images[ ].

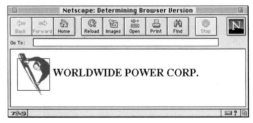

Table 11.4

mimeTypes Object	
PROPERTIES	
type	name of MIME type (e.g., image/jpeg)
description	MIME type description (e.g., JPEG image)
suffixes	MIME type suffixes (e.g., jpeg,jpg,jpe)
enabledPlugins	name of plug-in which handles MIME type

Script 11.7 You can use navigator to test the browser's MIME types.

```
script
<HTML>
<HEAD><TITLE>mimeTypes Example</TITLE></HEAD>
<BODY><CENTER><H1>ZETA STUDIOS<HR></H1>
<H2>CLIP: excerpt from
<I>The Making of JavaScript</I><BR><BR>
<SCRIPT LANGUAGE="JavaScript">
<!--HIDE
if (navigator.mimeTypes["video/quicktime"]) {
    document.write("<A HREF='making.mov'>Check
    →it out in Quicktime format</A>")
} else if (navigator.mimeTypes["video/mpeg"]) {
    document.write("<A HREF='making.mpg'>Check
    →it out in MPEG format</A>")
} else {
    document.write("To see the movie you need a
    →MPEG or quicktime helper application.")
}
//STOP HIDING-->
</SCRIPT></BODY></HTML>
```

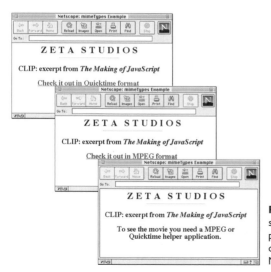

Figure 11.9 This script changes the page's link depending on the browser's MIME types.

Testing for a MIME Type

Browsers use helper applications and plug-ins to work with audio, video, and other complex files. These helpers use names called MIME *types* to describe what kinds of files they can work with.

With Navigator 3.0, you can use JavaScript to determine which plug-ins the user has and which MIME types the browser can handle. You can then use this information to customize your page. Script 11.7, for example, writes one of three different messages depending on what MIME types the browser supports.

To test for MIME types you use the mimeTypes array. Table 11.4 lists its properties.

To determine if the browser supports a MIME type:

```
if (navigator.mimeTypes["video/mpeg"]) {
document.write("<A HREF='making.mpg'>")}
```

1. if (   ) {
   document.write("<A HREF='making.mpg'>")}

   Create a conditional (see page 67), which will test for a MIME type and display a link to this type of file if the browser supports it.

2.   navigator.mimeTypes

   Type **navigator.mimeTypes** to address the array of MIME types.

3.   ["video/mpeg"]

   Specify the MIME type you want to test for within quotation marks and brackets. Script 11.7 tests for **video/mpeg** and **video/quicktime**.

DETERMINING THE PLUG-INS

Although you can create an exciting web page that uses plug-ins like Macromedia Shockwave and Adobe Amber, you can't be sure that the user will have them. With Navigator 3.0, you can test this information and only display your file to users who can see it.

You can do this with the plugins array. Table 11.5 lists its properties.

Determining the browser's plug-ins:

```
if (navigator.plugins["Quicktime"]) {
```

1. if ( ) {

Within your script, create a conditional (see page 67) that will test for a plug-in and display it on the page only if the browser can handle it.

2. navigator.plugins

Type **navigator.plugins** to address the array of plug-ins.

3. ["Quicktime"]

Follow **plugins** with the name of the plug-in you want to test for within quotation marks and brackets. Script 11.8 tests whether the user has Quicktime.

Table 11.5

plugins object	
PROPERTIES (ELEMENTS)	
name	name of the plug-in
filename	filename of the plug-in
description	plug-in's included self-description
mimeTypes	sub-array of mimeTypes the entry can handle

Script 11.8 You can determine which plug-ins the user's browser has.

```
<HTML>
<BODY><CENTER><H1>ZETA STUDIOS<HR></H1>
<H2>CLIP: excerpt from <I>The Making of
JavaScript</I><BR><BR></CENTER>
<SCRIPT LANGUAGE="JavaScript">
<!--HIDE
if (navigator.plugins["Quicktime"]) {
  document.write("<EMBED SRC='JS.MOV'
  →HEIGHT=100 WIDTH=100 ALIGN=LEFT HSPACE
  →=20></EMBED> <H3>It all began back at
  →Yale Law.</H3>")
} else {
  document.write("<IMAGE SRC='unhappy.gif'
  →ALIGN=LEFT HSPACE=20><H3>This page is
  →designed to run an in-line movie. Please
  →get a copy of Quicktime and reload this
  →page.")
}
//STOP HIDING-->
</SCRIPT></BODY></HTML>
```

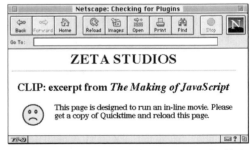

Figure 11.10 You can avoid showing your embedded movie to users who don't have the Quicktime plug-in.

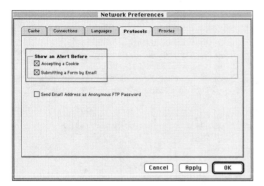

Figure 11.11 You can enable Navigator's cookie alert to observe the setting of cookies.

WHAT ARE COOKIES?

The information a web page stores normally disappears when the user quits her browser. To retain this information, many sites use registration names and save information on the server. Cookies provide a client-side alternative for keeping information between a user's visits.

When you create a cookie, JavaScript stores the text you give it on the user's hard drive. When the user comes back to your page your script can access this information. The remainder of this chapter explains how you can store, retrieve, and work with cookies.

There is no cookie object in JavaScript. Instead, you use the cookie property of **document** to access your pages entry on the user's hard drive. Because cookies contain text, you will often use the String object to work with them (see Chapter 6).

Navigator includes a preferences option which controls whether it displays a confirm dialog when setting a cookie (see Figure 11.11). Although you will generally want to leave this deactivated, you may want to enable it as you go through the examples on the following pages. This will allow you to see when your cookies are being set and what they contain.

STORING A COOKIE

When you want to store information, such as a preference setting, on the user's hard drive, you create a cookie. In doing this, you give it a name, some information to store, and, optionally, an expiration date and path. You put all of this into one long string and assign it to the cookie property.

To store a cookie:

```
document.cookie = "cookie1=" + str
+ ";expires=" + date + ";path=/"
```

1. **document.cookie =**

   Address the cookie property to access your document's entry on the user's hard drive. Type = to assign new information.

2. **"cookie1="**

   Within quotation marks, give your cookie a name and add =. The browser uses this name to determine if you are creating a new cookie or overwriting an old one.

3. **+ str**

   Type + followed by the text you want to store in parentheses or the name of a variable that stores this text.

4. **+ ";expires=" + date**

   Add ";expires=" to the string to show that you want to specify an expiration date. You use a semicolon to separate each part of the cookie. You can use a date variable to store the desired expiration time and convert it to a GMT string for use (see page 128). If you leave this off, the cookie will expire when the user quits his browser.

5. **+ ";path=/"**

   If you want other pages on your site to be able to see your cookie, type ";path=" and assign the file path that contains these pages (see Table 1.1). Script 11.9 uses a slash to let all pages on the site access the cookie.

Script 11.9 You can store a information on the user's hard drive in the form of cookies.

```
<HTML><HEAD><TITLE>Using Cookie</TITLE>
<SCRIPT LANGUAGE="JavaScript">
<!--HIDE
function storeIt(field) {
   var str = field.value
   var when = new Date()
   when.setMonth(when.getMonth() + 1)
   var date = when.toGMTString()
   document.cookie = "cookie1=" + str + ";
   →expires=" + date + ";path=/"
}
function getIt() {
   var str = unescape(document.cookie)
   var color = str.split("=")
   return color[1]
}
//STOP HIDING-->
</SCRIPT></HEAD>
<BODY BGCOLOR="&{getIt()};"><FORM>
Your Favorite Color:<INPUT TYPE="text"
→VALUE="&{getIt()};" onBlur="storeIt(this)">
</FORM></BODY></HTML>
```

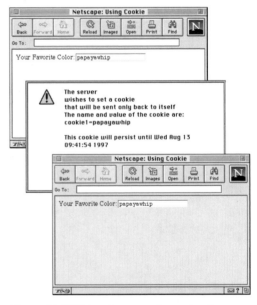

Figure 11.12 This script stores the user's color selection in a cookie and uses it as the background when he returns to the page.

Script 11.10 Document.cookie stores the names and values of a page's cookies.

```
<HTML><HEAD><TITLE>Retrieving Cookie</TITLE>
<SCRIPT LANGUAGE="JavaScript">
<!--HIDE
function storeIt(theForm) {
   var toCook = theForm.prod.selectedIndex +
   →":" + theForm.quant.value
   var when = new Date()
   when.setMonth(when.getMonth() + 1)
   document.cookie = "cooked=" + toCook + ";
   →expires=" + when.toGMTString()
}
function getIt(theForm) {
   if (document.cookie != "") {
      var save = document.cookie
      save = save.substring((save.indexOf("=")
      →+ 1),save.length)
      var cooks = save.split(":")
      theForm.prod.selectedIndex = cooks[0]
      theForm.quant.value = cooks[1]
   }
}
//STOP HIDING-->
</SCRIPT></HEAD>
<BODY onLoad="getIt(document.myForm)"
→onUnload="storeIt(document.myForm)">
<H1>Place your order!!</H1>
<FORM NAME="myForm"><H2>
Product: <SELECT SIZE=3 NAME="prod">
<OPTION>JavaScript Book</OPTION>
<OPTION>JavaScript T-Shirt</OPTION>
<OPTION>Life size poster of Ted and Jeremy
</OPTION></SELECT><BR>
<BR>Quantity:
<INPUT TYPE="text" SIZE=3 VALUE=1 NAME="quant">
<BR><BR><INPUT TYPE="submit">
</FORM></BODY></HTML>
```

Figure 11.13 This script stores and retrieves the user's choices with a cookie.

RETRIEVING A COOKIE

Once you've set a cookie, you use **cookie** to access it when the user returns to your page.

The information you get back from a cookie is a bit different than what you store. JavaScript doesn't bother telling you the expiration date or path of the cookie. Instead, it gives you the name followed by an equals sign and the text you stored. Because you usually don't care what the name of your cookie is, you will generally want to isolate the stored text before you can work with it.

To retrieve a cookie:

1. if (document.cookie != "") {

Within a function, create a conditional (see page 67) to test whether a cookie has been set. To do this, test if **cookie** contains a null string (""). If it does not, your script can work with the stored information.

2. var save = document.cookie

Within the conditional, create a new variable and use = to assign it the information in the cookie.

3. save = save.substring((save.indexOf("=") + 1), save.length)

Use **substring()** (see page 86) to remove the name and equals sign from your cookie so that you can work with the text.

4. var cooks = save.split(":")

If you want to store more than one piece of information in a cookie, you should separate each with a colon. When you access the cookie, you can use **split()** (see page 89), to make each piece of information an entry in a new array. This makes it much easier to work with individual parts of the cookie.

ENCODING PUNCTUATION

Because the browser uses commas, semi-colons, and spaces to separate the parts of the cookie, you cannot put these in the text you store. To get around this, you can convert these to special codes which represent them.

JavaScript makes this easy. To convert the illegal characters you use **escape()**; to restore them, you use **unescape()**.

To encode punctuation in a cookie:

1. var str = escape(raw)

var str =

Within your script, create a variable to store the converted text for your cookie.

escape

Type **escape** to tell JavaScript that you want to convert the punctuation in your string into its equivalent codes.

(raw)

Within parentheses, type the name of the variable that stores the text for your cookie.

2. document.cookie = "cookie1=" + str + "; expires=" + theDate.toGMTString()

Store your converted text in a cookie, as described on page 158. The punctuation will be encoded as in Figure 11.14.

3. var raw = unescape(str)

var raw =

When you want to work with the text in its original state, create a new variable to store the unencoded version for later use.

unescape(str)

To reinsert the punctuation, type **unescape** followed by the name of the variable which stores the cookie's text in parentheses.

Script 11.11 You need to use the escape and unescape functions to encode spaces, commas, and semicolons in your cookies.

```
<HTML><HEAD><TITLE>Encoding Cookies</TITLE>
<SCRIPT LANGUAGE="JavaScript">
<!--HIDE
function storeIt() {
  var theDate=new Date()
  theDate.setMonth(theDate.getMonth() + 1)
  var raw = document.forms[0]elements[0].value
  var str = escape(raw)
  document.cookie = "cookie1=" + str +
  ⇥"; expires=" + theDate.toGMTString()
}
function getIt() {
  if (document.cookie != "") {
    var str = document.cookie
    var first = str.split("=")
    str = first[1]
    var raw = unescape(str)
    document.forms[0].elements[0].value = raw
  }
}
//STOP HIDING-->
</SCRIPT></HEAD>
<BODY onUnload="storeIt()" onLoad="getIt()">
<IMG SRC="home.gif" ALIGN=left>
<BR><H1>World Power Corporation Client-Side
Database</H1><BR>
<FORM>Name:<INPUT TYPE="text" SIZE=50><BR>
</FORM></BODY></HTML>
```

Figure 11.14 This script converts the punctuation in the user's name into codes for storage.

Script 11.12 You can use a separate cookie for each form element.

```
<HTML><HEAD>
<TITLE>multiple cookies</TITLE>
<SCRIPT LANGUAGE="JavaScript">
<!--HIDE
var arr
function cookieMonster() {
  arr=new Array(document.forms[0].length)
  var theDate=new Date()
  theDate.setMonth(theDate.getMonth()+1)
  for (i=0;i<document.forms[0].length;i++) {
    arr[i]="cookie" + i
    document.cookie=arr[i]+ "=" + document
    →.forms[0].elements[i].value + "; expires
    →="+ theDate.toGMTString()
  }
}
function getIt() {
  var str=document.cookie
  if (str != "") {
    var str1=str.split(";")
    for (i=0;i<str1.length;i++) {
      var pivot=str1[i].split("=")
      document.forms[0].elements[i]
      →.value=pivot[1]
    }
  }
}
//STOP HIDING-->
</SCRIPT> </HEAD> <BODY onLoad="getIt()"
→onUnload="cookieMonster()"><FORM>
<H2>Enter all sorts of data:</H2>
<INPUT TYPE="text"><BR>
<INPUT TYPE="text"><BR>
<INPUT TYPE="text"><BR>
</FORM></BODY></HTML>
```

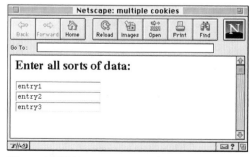

Figure 11.15 Using separate cookies, you can save the value of twenty form elements on a site.

STORING MULTIPLE COOKIES

You can store an enormous amount of information in a single cookie, but it can get complicated trying to break down a long string into the parts you need. Instead, it's often easier to make a separate cookie for each piece of information, as in Script 11.12. You should keep in mind, however, that you can only use twenty cookies per path.

To store user input in multiple cookies:

1. arr=new Array(document.forms[0].length)

   arr=new Array(   )

   Within a function triggered when the document loads, create an array to store your cookies' names (see page 131).

   document.forms[0].length

   Address the form you want to save and type **.length**. This way, your array will have one entry for each form element.

2. for (i=0;i<document.forms[0].length;i++) {

   Define a for loop which will repeat for each entry in your form (see page 74).

3. arr[i] = "cookie" + i

   As the first statement of your loop, type your array name followed by the counter within braces. Assign each entry **"cookie"** followed by your counter variable so that the entry stores the cookie's name.

4. document.cookie = arr[i] + "=" +
   document.forms[0].elements[i].value

   document.cookie = arr[i] + "=" +

   Assign an array entry and the equals sign to **document.cookie**. This creates a cookie for each form element.

   document.forms[0].elements[i].value

   Use the counter variable to address the correct form element and fill the cookie with its value.

DELETING A COOKIE

Sometimes you'll want to use a cookie to track a user's progress through your site or, as in Script 11.13, to count the user's visits to your site. To reset this information you'll need to delete your cookies.

Your browser automatically checks the cookies that it has stored and deletes the ones whose expiration date has passed. By changing its expiration date to the current time, you can delete a cookie instantly.

To delete a cookie:

1. var now = new Date()

Store the current date in a variable with the Date constructor (see page 124).

2. document.cookie = "visits=;expires=" + now.toGMTString()

document.cookie =

Type **document.cookie** and the equals sign to assign a cookie for your page.

"visits=;

Type a quotation mark followed by the name of the cookie that you want to delete, an equals sign, and a semicolon. This tells the browser to overwrite the old cookie. Don't bother giving it text.

expires="

Type **expires=** and a quotation mark to give your cookie a new expiration date.

+ now.toGMTString()

Type the name of your date variable and **.toGMTString()** (see page 128) to specify the current time as the new expiration date. This makes the browser delete the cookie immediately.

Script 11.13 You can delete a cookie by setting its expiration date to the present time.

```
<HTML>
<HEAD><TITLE>Deleting a Cookie</TITLE>
<SCRIPT LANGUAGE="JavaScript">
<!--HIDE
function visitCount() {
  var then = new Date()
  var count = 0
  var str=document.cookie
  if (document.cookie !="") {
    var str1 = str.split("=")
    count = eval(str1[1])
  }
  alert("You've visited " + count + " times.")
  count += 1
  then.setMonth(then.getMonth() + 1)
  document.cookie = "visits=" + count +
  →"; expires=" + then.toGMTString()
}
function deleteIt() {
  var now = new Date()
  document.cookie = "visits=; expires="+
  →now.toGMTString()
}
//STOP HIDING-->
</SCRIPT></HEAD>
<BODY onLoad="visitCount()"><FORM>
<INPUT TYPE="button" VALUE="Reset Visit Record"
→onClick="deleteIt()">
</FORM></BODY></HTML>
```

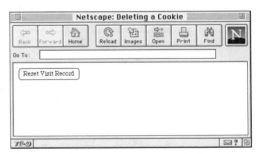

Figure 11.16 When the user presses the Reset button, this script deletes the cookie, resetting the visitation record.

JAVA AND JAVASCRIPT

Lots of pages on the World Wide Web now use Java applets and plug-ins, which do things that HTML and JavaScript simply cannot. As great as these new technologies are, however, their abilities don't extend beyond their borders on the page.

With Navigator 3.0, you can use JavaScript to communicate with Java applets and plug-ins, enabling them to work with all parts of the page. This new feature is called LiveConnect. You can use it to control any files embedded in your page.

Although it's difficult to know what role LiveConnect will play in the future, it's sure to be big. LiveConnect will expand the potential of the Web by creating new interactive possibilities.

DETERMINING IF JAVA IS ENABLED

Navigator allows the user to turn Java and JavaScript on and off with the dialog shown in Figure 12.2. If the user does not have Java enabled, you should tell her to turn it on and leave the applets out of your page, as in Script 12.1.

You can use javaEnabled() to perform this test.

To provide alternate content if Java is not enabled:

1. if (navigator.javaEnabled()) {

   if (   ) {

   Create a conditional within your script (see page 70) to determine whether the user has Java turned on.

   navigator.javaEnabled()

   Type navigator.javaEnabled() as its condition. This will return **true** if Java is turned on and **false** if it isn't.

2. document.write("<APPLET CODE= TicTacToe.class WIDTH=120 HEIGHT=120> </APPLET>")

   document.write("
                  ")

   Type document.write() (see page 11) as the first statement of your conditional.

   <APPLET CODE= TicTacToe.class WIDTH=120 HEIGHT=120>

   Write the applet tag to insert your Java applet.

   </APPLET>

   Write </APPLET> to end your applet.

3. } else { document.write("This page contains a Java applet") }

   Use an else statement (see page 70) to display a message if the user doesn't have Java enabled, as in Figure 12.1.

Script 12.1 You use javaEnabled() to determine whether Java is turned on or off.

```
script

<HTML><HEAD>
<TITLE>javaEnabled() Example</TITLE></HEAD>
<BODY><CENTER>
<H2>JAVA TIC-TAC-TOE<HR WIDTH=40%><BR><BR>
<SCRIPT LANGUAGE="JavaScript">
<!--HIDE
if (navigator.javaEnabled()) {
   document.write("<APPLET CODE=TicTacToe.class
   →WIDTH=120 HEIGHT=120></APPLET>")
} else {
   document.write("This page contains a Java
   →applet. Please enable Java in the Network
   →Preferences dialog box.")
}
//STOP HIDING-->
</SCRIPT></H2></CENTER></BODY></HTML>
```

Figure 12.1 The left page appears if the user doesn't have Java enabled, the right one if she does.

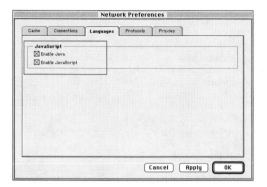

Figure 12.2 To activate LiveConnect, select both Java and JavaScript in the Network Preferences dialog.

USING LIVECONNECT

LiveConnect allows scripts, applets, and plug-ins to access one another. As a result, you can now use JavaScript to trigger functions in applets and plug-ins. You can also trigger methods which are built into Java itself.

To turn on LiveConnect, enable both Java and JavaScript in Navigator's Network Preferences dialog box (see Figure 12.2). To test if the user has both of these turned on, you can use **javaEnabled()**, as described on the previous page.

When LiveConnect is active, JavaScript can access applets and plug-ins through three objects: **Packages[ ]**, **applets[ ]**, and **embeds[ ]**.

You use **Packages[ ]** to address the Java hierarchy. By doing this, you can trigger Java methods within your script.

You use **applets[ ]** to access the applets on your page. By doing this, you can trigger functions defined in the applet.

You use **embeds[ ]** to access plug-in functions for the files embedded on your page.

USING A JAVA METHOD

If you want your script to do something only possible in Java, you can call the appropriate Java method from JavaScript. In order to use this technique you'll have to know a little about Java, or at least how to address the command you want.

Once you know the Java address of your command you can access it from JavaScript through the Packages object, which contains the three main Java packages: **sun**, **netscape**, and **java**.

To use a Java method:

1. Open the Java console, a window where Java applets can display information. In Navigator you do this by selecting Show Java Console from the Options menu.

2. Packages.java.lang.System.err.print("greetings from JavaScript")

    Packages

    Within your script, wherever you want to call the Java method, type **Packages** to tell JavaScript you are going to be using a Java command.

    > .java.lang.System.err.print("greetings from JavaScript")

    Type a dot followed the address of the Java command you want to use. Java's object hierarchy is beyond the scope of this book. As you can see from Figure 12.3, however, .java.lang.System.err.print() puts the message you give it in the Java console.

Script 12.2 Your script can use Java methods.

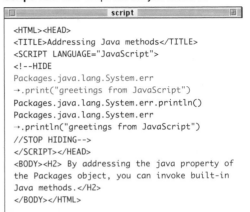

```
<HTML><HEAD>
<TITLE>Addressing Java methods</TITLE>
<SCRIPT LANGUAGE="JavaScript">
<!--HIDE
Packages.java.lang.System.err
→.print("greetings from JavaScript")
Packages.java.lang.System.err.println()
Packages.java.lang.System.err
→.println("greetings from JavaScript")
//STOP HIDING-->
</SCRIPT></HEAD>
<BODY><H2> By addressing the java property of
the Packages object, you can invoke built-in
Java methods.</H2>
</BODY></HTML>
```

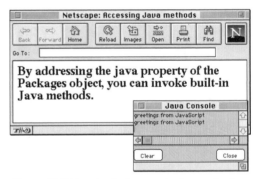

Figure 12.3 Here JavaScript uses the Java methods print() and println() to write to the Java console.

Script 12.3 You can access and change the parts of Java applets.

```
<HTML>
<HEAD><TITLE>Controlling an Applet</TITLE>
<SCRIPT LANGUAGE="JavaScript">
<!--HIDE
var i = 9
function changeIt(change) {
  if ((i + change) > 0) {
    i += change
  }
  document.applets[0].speed = i
}
//STOP HIDING-->
</SCRIPT></HEAD>
<BODY><CENTER>
<APPLET code=Ticker.class width=400 height=35>
<PARAM name=msg0 value="<-- Buy our JavaScript
→book --- ">
<PARAM name=msg1 value="Buy a JavaScript T-
→Shirt --- ">
<PARAM name=speed value=9>
</APPLET>
<BR><FORM>
<INPUT TYPE="button" VALUE="<< SLOWER"
→onClick="changeIt(-2)">
<INPUT TYPE="button" VALUE="FASTER >>"
→onClick="changeIt(2)">
</CENTER></BODY></HTML>
```

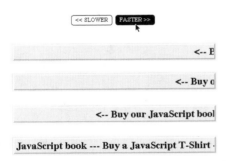

Figure 12.4 Each time the user clicks on a button, JavaScript changes the value of the Java variable that determines scroll speed.

ACCESSING A JAVA APPLET

If there is a Java applet on the same page as your script, you can access it and change the way it functions. Script 12.3, for example, changes a variable in a Java ticker applet to make the text scroll faster or slower.

To do this you'll need to look at the code for the applet you want to work with. This is often freely available on the same site you find the applet itself. Once you've got the code, look for variables labeled **public**; these are the ones you can access. You can often tell what a variable controls by its name and the author's comments.

You can address the parts of a Java applet through the applets array or by the name you give them in the applet tag.

To access a Java applet:

document.applets[0].speed = i

1. document.applets[ ]

Within your script, address the applets array.

2.   0

Within the brackets, type the index number of the applet you want to access. The first one on the page is number zero.

3.   .speed

Type a dot followed by the name of the Java variable that you want to access or change.

OR   .changeSpeed(i)

If you want to call a function in the applet, type a dot followed by its name and parentheses. You can give it information from your script as an argument.

4.   = i

To change a Java variable, use the equals sign to assign it a new value.

CONTROLLING A PLUG-IN

If you are working with a plug-in, you can use JavaScript to let the user control it with form elements. Script 12.4, for example, includes an embedded file for the Envoy plug-in. The script allows the user to change the magnification, move to a different page, and search for text. You can create this type of script by addressing the plug-in through embeds[ ].

To control a plug-in:

onChange="document.embeds[0].setZoom (parseInt(this.value))"

1. onChange="
　　　　"

Insert an event handler in the desired HTML tag (see page 32). Script 12.4 reacts to changes in the page's text fields.

2. 　　　　　document.embeds[ ]

Address the embeds array.

3. 　　　　　　　　　　　　0

Within the brackets, type the number of the embedded plug-in file that you want to access. The first embed tag on the page is number zero.

4. 　　　　　　　　　　　　.setZoom

Type a dot followed by the name of the plug-in function that you want to use. You can find out what commands are available at the company's web site.

5. (parseInt(this.value))

Within parentheses, type the information that you want to pass to the plug-in. In Script 12.4, this is a number specifying the zoom percentage. The plug-in's instructions will describe what kinds of information you should give it.

Script 12.4 You can access certain plug-in functions through your script.

```
<HTML><HEAD>
<TITLE>Controlling a Plug-in</TITLE></HEAD>
<BODY><CENTER>
<EMBED NAME="theDoc" SRC="wowser.evy" WIDTH=250
→HEIGHT=400 BORDER=1 PLUGINSPAGE=
→"http://www.twcorp.com/plugin.htm">
<BR>
<FORM>
Zoom: <INPUT TYPE="text" SIZE=3 VALUE="100"
→onChange="document.embeds[0].setZoom
→(parseInt(this.value))">%
Go to page: <INPUT TYPE="text" SIZE=3
→VALUE="1" onChange="document.theDoc
→.setCurrentPage(parseInt(this.value) - 1)">
<BR>
Find text: <INPUT TYPE="text" SIZE=20
→onChange="document.embeds[0].findText(this
→.value, true, false)">
</FORM></BODY></HTML>
```

APPENDIX: OBJECT HIERARCHY

A

JavaScript organizes nearly all of its tools into a hierarchy based on the structure of the browser. Learning this is the most important step in mastering JavaScript.

This appendix provides a complete listing of all the objects supported by Navigator 3.0. The properties, methods, and event handlers for each object are shown beside it and are separated by the symbols explained in the chart at the bottom of page 170.

Pages 170–171 contain a visual map of the hierarchical objects, beginning at the left of the first page and ending at the right of the second. By following this map, you can determine the complete address of any property or method.

Page 172 lists the objects outside of the hierarchy, which JavaScript uses to provide useful information unrelated to the browser. Because JavaScript gives each frame its own hierarchy, we have listed the frame object separately, on page 172.

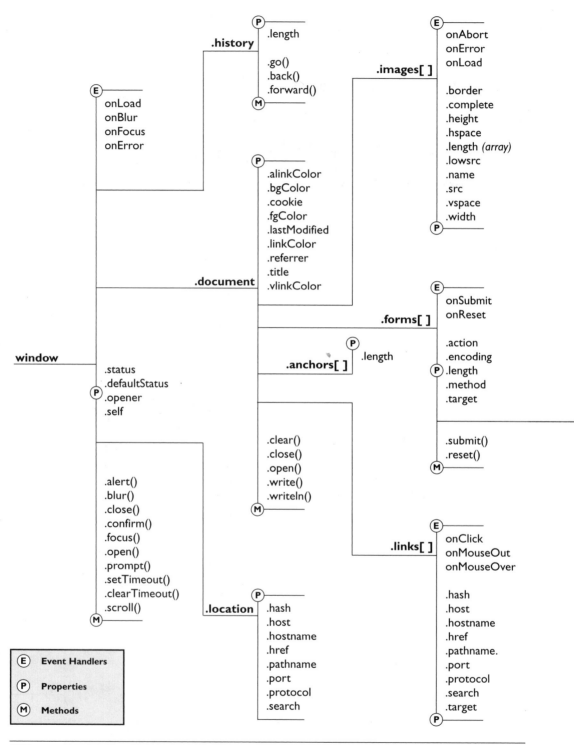

.history
- P .length
- .go()
- .back()
- .forward() M

.images[ ]
- E onAbort
- onError
- onLoad
- .border
- .complete
- .height
- .hspace
- .length *(array)*
- .lowsrc
- .name
- .src
- .vspace
- .width P

E
- onLoad
- onBlur
- onFocus
- onError

.document
- P .alinkColor
- .bgColor
- .cookie
- .fgColor
- .lastModified
- .linkColor
- .referrer
- .title
- .vlinkColor

.forms[ ]
- E onSubmit
- onReset
- .action
- .encoding
- P .length
- .method
- .target

.anchors[ ]
- P .length

window
- P .status
- .defaultStatus
- .opener
- .self

- .clear()
- .close()
- .open()
- .write()
- .writeln() M

- .submit()
- .reset() M

- .alert()
- .blur()
- .close()
- .confirm()
- .focus()
- .open()
- .prompt()
- .setTimeout()
- .clearTimeout()
- .scroll() M

.links[ ]
- E onClick
- onMouseOut
- onMouseOver
- .hash
- .host
- .hostname
- .href
- .pathname.
- .port
- .protocol
- .search
- .target P

.location
- P .hash
- .host
- .hostname
- .href
- .pathname
- .port
- .protocol
- .search

- E Event Handlers
- P Properties
- M Methods

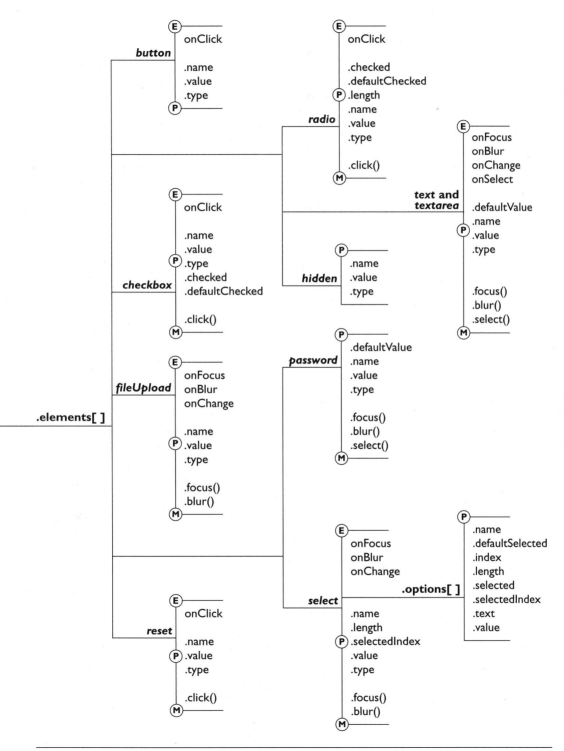

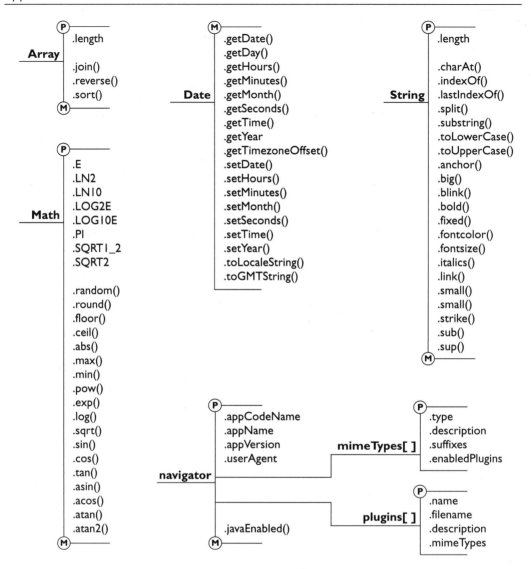

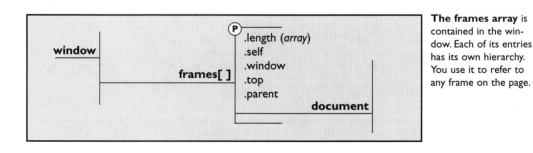

The frames array is contained in the window. Each of its entries has its own hierarchy. You use it to refer to any frame on the page.

APPENDIX: NAVIGATOR 3.0

Navigator 3.0's version of JavaScript, called JavaScript 1.1, is a far more complete and reliable language than that of 2.0. This appendix indexes the new features and those original features which have been significantly changed, and tells you where these features are covered in the book.

If you learned JavaScript with Navigator 2.0, you can use this appendix to bring yourself fully up to date. Each new and changed feature is listed with a page reference. Notes indicate how changed features differ from Navigator 2.0.

It is good policy to make a page perform to the best of the ability of the user's browser. This means including work-arounds for those users with Navigator 2.0. If you are using the features listed in this appendix, you should test the user's browser (see page 154) and provide alternative code for those not equipped with the latest version.

New to Navigator 3.0

APPENDIX: INTERNET EXPLORER

Microsoft has added JavaScript support to Internet Explorer 3.0. Although Microsoft calls its version JScript, it is basically the same as JavaScript in Navigator 2.0.

The list on the following page describes the principle differences between these two versions. It also includes cases where JScript supports Navigator 3.0 features.

If you want your pages to be viewable by the maximum number of viewers, you will want to pay attention to these differences. You can use this appendix to make your pages compatible with both browsers.

Internet Explorer 3.0

defaultValue

Explorer does not support **defaultValue** for text fields or text blocks. An attempt to use it will cause an error. See page 52.

document.cookie

Explorer does not support cookies. If you attempt to access **cookie**, you will get an empty string, but it will not cause an error. See page 157.

document.forms[0].encoding

Explorer does not support this property, but it will not cause an error. See page 60.

document.links[0]

Explorer's link properties are read-only. An attempt to change them will not cause an error. See page 106.

history.length

In Explorer, this property always stores zero. See page 148.

Math.random()

Although it does not work in Navigator 2.0, **random()** works properly in Explorer 3.0. See page 91.

onMouseOver

In Explorer, this event handler will not work within a form. See page 108.

window.navigate("URL")

Navigate() moves the window to the URL you specify. This is the equivalent of assigning a URL to **window.location** in Navigator. See page 149.

window.opener

Although this property is not supported in Navigator 2.0, it works properly in Explorer 3.0. See page 139.

‹SCRIPT FOR="buttonName" event="onClick"›

To replace an event handler in Explorer, you can place this line directly after the form element you wish to script. This technique can be used with any form element or link and any relevant event handler. See page 31.

INDEX